BARBECUE and SUMMER PARTY COOKBOOK

GUILD PUBLISHING
LONDON

Editor: Julia Canning
Art Editor: Brenda Morrison
Production: Richard Churchill

This edition published 1985 by Book Club Associates
by arrangement with Windward, an imprint owned by
W. H. Smith & Son Limited
Registered No. 237811 England
Trading as WHS Distributors,
St John's House, East Street, Leicester LE1 6NE

Printed and bound in Hong Kong by Dai Nippon Printing Company

INTRODUCTION

The *Barbecue and Summer Party Cookbook* guides you through all sorts of summertime occasions, from impromptu barbecues to lavish dinner parties. With our wide choice of delectable recipes and interesting menu suggestions, you will be amazed at how effortless summer cooking can be! Our aim is that you, the cook, should be free to enjoy the carefree mood of summer as much as your guests.

Barbecuing is a wonderful way to eat outdoors — few people can resist the aroma of sizzling barbecued meat. And, best of all, the cooking is simple: in fact, everyone can lend a hand! Our barbecue section gives you all the know-how you need to cut the guesswork out of cooking over coals — and there are lots of unusual accompaniment ideas that will make your barbecue that bit more sophisticated. Together with a variety of imaginative barbecue recipes — ranging from colourful kebabs to tasty stuffed fish — and three original party menus, you can add a whole new dimension to your barbecue skills.

Bright, sunny weather is a great incentive for holding parties. To encourage this sociable mood, we give a selection of party planners for outdoor and indoor entertaining. The outdoor menus range from casual affairs, such as a family picnic and a delicious brunch, to more lavish spreads — our glamorous patio party and a mouth-watering buffet dinner party are most impressive. If you entertain indoors, capture the sunny mood of summer with a laid-back Californian meal, or try adding a touch of spice with a curry lunch. Planned down to the last detail, our party menus ensure that you can entertain with ease.

Summer would not be the same without salads, and our salad section gives you lots of original ideas for summer meals. Colourful and full of fresh flavour, the salads range from crisp starters to satisfying main course meals. Drinks parties, whether based on exciting cocktails or cool punches, are sure to go down well in the summer. Our exciting drinks party menus offer a selection of knock-out alcoholic thirst quenchers and a wide choice of nibbles to serve with them.

All the recipes in this book are fully illustrated and are set out in an easy-to-follow style, so that you can't possibly go wrong. And that's not all, each recipe also has a panel of handy cook's notes, providing all the hints you've ever wanted to know — there are tips on preparation, serving ideas and even a buying guide. What more could you need!

CONTENTS

BARBECUES

SUMMER ENTERTAINING

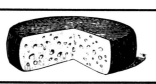

BARBECUES
KNOW-HOW

Barbecues are a must for summer — cooking outdoors is great fun and everyone loves the flavour of barbecued food. With a little barbecue know-how, you can soon become an expert at this form of cooking: family and friends alike will be delighted at the delicious results!

Basic equipment

There are many portable barbecues which can be bought or hired. Models range from table-height appliances, complete with hoods, to small 'table top' ones, perfect for a picnic or use on a balcony. More elaborate models may incorporate a warming oven shelf or rôtisserie spit.

Alternatively, you can improvise by building your own barbecue with bricks or by using a heatproof container, such as a garden refuse burner. All you really need is a hole for the draught, to keep the fire burning, and a grid — oven shelves make ideal grids. A permanent brick structure is particularly good if you barbecue on a regular basis and, depending on the materials used, can also save you money.

Accessories

Long-handled barbecue tool sets, which usually comprise tongs, a spatula and a two-pronged fork, are vital for easy handling of food — and for safety. You will also need a long-handled brush for brushing oil or marinade on to the food to keep it moist during cooking, and oven gloves for protecting your hands.

For kebabs, choose flat skewers with sharp points: the food can be turned over more efficiently. A hinged wire grill or basket is ideal for fish, because each side is enclosed by a wire mesh and the double handle enables you to turn the fish without breaking up the flesh.

Paper napkins and absorbent paper are useful for mopping up, while paper plates and disposable table cloths make clearing up easier. Plasters and antiseptic cream are good to have to hand, in case of emergencies, and covers for the food may be needed if insects prove to be a problem.

Site

Site the barbecue within easy reach of the house, but away from overhanging trees, bushes and long grasses. Make sure that it is completely stable, too. Charcoal gives off carbon monoxide, so do not use in a confined space.

Fuel

Some of the more sophisticated models are run on gas or electricity, but the usual fuel is charcoal. Charcoal can be bought in bags from hardware shops, garden centres and larger supermarkets. Briquettes are more expensive than ordinary pieces of lumpwood charcoal, but they usually burn for longer and are therefore more economical in the long run. They are also less messy and, since they are regular in shape, produce a uniform heat without sparks.

For more impromtu, camp-fire style barbecues, hardwood — oak, ash, beech or fruit wood — is traditionally used as fuel.

Lighting the barbecue

Light the barbecue 45-60 minutes before you intend to cook. This will give the charcoal time to stop burning and become red and glowing.

The simplest way to light the charcoal is to mound it up in a pyramid in the centre of the barbecue and insert some solid firelighters in between the charcoal. Barbecue lighting fluid can also be used — it is very efficient; so too are special electric or gas barbecue pokers, but they are expensive and only worth buying if you intend to do a lot of barbecuing.

Do not be tempted to use any highly inflammable liquid, such as petrol, paraffin or lighter fluid, to light the fire or give it a boost — apart from the obvious danger, any of these might give the food an unpleasant taste.

When the flames have subsided and the coals look grey in the daylight or glow red in the dark, spread the coals out in a single layer and start cooking.

Cooking over coals

It is preferable to oil the grid before cooking, but take care not to drip any oil on the coals, as this will cause a flare up. Oiling the grid helps to prevent the food from sticking to the grid. As a general rule, the grid should be positioned 7.5 cm/3 inches above the hot coals.

The heat of the barbecue can be controlled in several ways. In some barbecues air vents can be opened or closed to vary the amount of draught, or the grid can be moved nearer to or further from the fire. Alternatively, move items that have cooked before others, to the outer edges of the grid. To concentrate the heat, heap up the coals, and to damp it down, spread the coals further apart. If you need to add more fuel, allow the new charcoal to warm up gradually around the edge of the fire pan, then push it in towards the centre as it heats up.

Smoke flavouring: to create a woody flavour, add dampened pieces of wood to the hot coals. Try fruit woods with chicken and fish, and hardwoods for sausages and steaks. Packets of specially prepared wood chips, usually hickory or apple, are available; or dried rosemary branches produce a particularly delicate flavour. Do not use resinous woods, such as pine, since they give an unpleasant flavour.

Add fresh herbs, garlic cloves and orange zest to the coals during the last few minutes of cooking, to create exotic aromatic smoke. Rosemary or thyme is particularly good with lamb.

Flare ups: these are the flames that shoot up from the coals when meat fat drips on to them. Uncontrolled, these flames will burn your food to a crisp. As a precaution against flare ups, never put meat on the barbecue before the coals are glowing, and trim meat of excess fat before cooking it. If flare ups still occur, just douse the flames with a fine spray of water — always have a filled water sprinkler to hand.

Barbecuing meat
The simplest way to cook meat is to place it directly on a grid over the hot coals. Always bring meat to room temperature before barbecuing — chilled meat will be overdone on the outside before it has had a chance to cook on the inside.

Steaks and chops: in general, these small cuts should be about 4 cm/ 1½ inches thick. Pork chops should be thinner, as pork must always be cooked right through. Large rump, fillet and sirloin steaks can be cooked in one piece and then cut into thick slices for serving — in this way less juice will be lost.

Trim most of the fat from steaks and chops, to avoid flare ups, then make small cuts around the remaining fat to prevent the meat curling.

Chicken pieces: barbecue chicken halves bone-side down first — the bones act as heat conductors and speed up the cooking. It is often quicker to partly cook the chicken in the oven before barbecuing.

Larger joints: although joints, such as beef ribs and legs of lamb, can be cooked on the grid (if turned and basted frequently), spit roasting is really the ideal way to barbecue whole poultry or large joints of meat. Make sure that the spit is pushed through the centre of the meat and check that the meat is evenly balanced so that it cooks evenly. Heap the hot coals at one side of the spit and put a drip pan beneath the meat. This will prevent the fat from making the fire too fierce.

Burgers: beefburgers — as well as lamb and pork burgers — are always popular. If you are worried about home-made ones breaking up, place them on an oiled heated metal tray on top of the grid.

Kebabs: these are a good way of barbecuing the cheaper cuts of meat, such as shoulder of lamb and hand of pork, although better quality meat, offal and boned poultry are equally suitable. Cut the meat into 2.5 cm/1 inch squares and thread on to skewers, alternating with vegetables. Turn frequently.

Foil cooking: a foil wrapping seals in flavour and juices. This is a particularly good way to barbecue small cuts of lean meat, gammon steaks and firm German-type sausages. Brush the meat lightly with oil, scatter it with herbs and sliced onion, wrap in a double layer of foil and place the parcel on the grid.

Barbecuing fish and shellfish
Small and large fish can be grilled whole. Large fish can also be cut into steaks or fillets, but small fillets will cook too quickly in the fierce heat of a barbecue. Thick, firm fillets, such as those of cod or swordfish, can also be cubed for kebabs. Fish is much easier to handle if you put it in a hinged wire grill or basket.

Unshelled cooked prawns can be marinated, then heated through for a short time on the grid. Barbecuing is also a good way to cook freshly killed lobster.

Marinades
Marinating greatly improves the flavour of most cuts of meat; it will also help to tenderize tougher meats, such as the cheaper cuts used for kebabs. Marinating fish will keep the flesh moist while it is cooking.

Accompaniments
Sauces are best made indoors before the party, but they can be kept warm on the edge of the grid.

Potatoes wrapped in foil and placed directly in the hot coals go well with barbecued meat and fish. You can also cook whole, large potatoes on the grid; brush them lightly with oil, and barbecue for at least 1½ hours, turning occasionally.

If you fancy fried potatoes, lay a shallow pan, containing a mixture of oil and butter, on the grid. Slice unpeeled potatoes into the hot fat and fry them until they are evenly browned and tender. Small new potatoes can be wrapped, together with a sprinkling of finely chopped parsley, in a double layer of well-buttered foil and cooked over the coals on the grid.

Vegetable parcels: other vegetables are also very successful cooked in foil parcels. Mushrooms can be thinly sliced and wrapped up with a sprinkling of lemon juice and fresh herbs. Try peas, fresh or frozen, with a spoonful of double cream spooned over them, or broad beans with a knob of butter and a sprinkling of herbs.

Carrots and other root vegetables are excellent cut into thin matchstick strips, while courgettes are good sliced or cooked whole. Make parcels of whole corn on the cobs or small peeled onions − these are delicious with the addition of some flavoured butter.

Hot bread: always goes down well at barbecue parties; wrap whole loaves, pitta bread or rolls in foil and heat through on a rack about 35 cm/14 inches from the hot coals, while the other food is cooking.

For garlic bread, cut a French loaf diagonally into slices, about 5 cm/2 inches thick, slicing to the bottom of the loaf but not cutting through it. Spread the cut surfaces with 175 g/6 oz soft butter mixed with 2 garlic cloves crushed, then reform into a loaf shape. Wrap in foil and heat on the grid for about 20 minutes, or until the loaf is crisp.

For herbed bread, repeat as for garlic bread, but replace the garlic with ½ teaspoon each of dried marjoram, parsley and chives or 2 tablespoons of fresh herbs.

Barbecuing fruit
Take advantage of the remaining fire, when the main course is over, to cook fruit. Firm fruit can be cubed, brushed with a spiced sugar or honey syrup and made into kebabs. Try using combinations of dessert apples and pears; pineapple, apricots and peaches.

Try cooking fruit in foil; stuff apples and pears with mincemeat, then wrap in a double layer of buttered foil and cook on the grid for about 45 minutes, turning occasionally. Alternatively, put the foil parcels directly into the grey ashes and cook for 15-30 minutes. Or combine sliced fruit with spices, dried fruit, brown sugar and honey and cook in foil on the grid for 30 minutes.

Bananas are perfect for barbecuing. For an unusual dessert, place whole bananas in their skins on the grid and cook over the coals for about 15 minutes until the skins are black: serve slit open with single cream and liqueur poured over the revealed flesh. Another idea is to slit the skins of whole bananas, remove the bananas, brush with warmed honey and spices and put them back in their skins. Wrap in foil and cook over the coals for 15 minutes. For another variation, slit the bananas and fill them with grated chocolate, rum butter or diced marshmallows before returning them to their skins or, alternatively, to thin foil parcels.

RECIPES

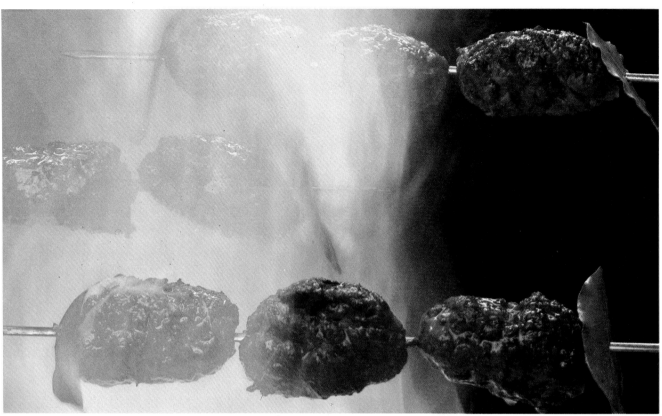

Minced beef kebabs

SERVES 4
500 g/1 lb lean minced beef (see
   Buying guide)
1 onion, very finely chopped
1 clove garlic, finely chopped
   (optional)
1 egg, beaten
2 tablespoons natural yoghurt
1 tablespoon chopped fresh parsley
½ teaspoon ground cinnamon
salt and freshly ground black pepper
vegetable oil, for brushing
bay leaves, to garnish

1 Put all the ingredients except the
oil and bay leaves in a large bowl
and mix together with a fork.
2 Cover the bowl and refrigerate
the mixture for 1 hour.
3 Light the barbecue.
4 Divide the mixture into 12 equal
portions. Shape each portion into a

'sausage' about 5 cm/2 inches long,
squeezing each sausage firmly between the hands, to make it as
compact as possible. [!]
5 Brush 4 kebab skewers with oil.
Push a bay leaf on to the end of each
skewer. Then push 3 'sausages' on
to each skewer, moulding them
firmly round the skewers so that

they remain securely in place. [!]
Finish each skewer with a bay leaf.
6 When the coals are hot, brush
kebabs all over with oil and place on
the grid. Cook the kebabs over the
hot coals for 7-10 minutes, [!] turning frequently. Transfer the kebabs
to individual dinner plates and
serve at once.

Cook's Notes

TIME
25 minutes preparation
and cooking, plus 1
hour chilling.

 DID YOU KNOW
This recipe is a version
of a very popular Mid-
dle Eastern dish – *kofta* kebabs
(skewered meat balls).

 BUYING GUIDE
Buy the best-quality
minced beef for this re-
cipe. The very finely minced

meat sold in supermarkets as
'ground beef' is ideal.

[!] WATCHPOINTS
If the 'sausages' are too
large the skewers will
not support their weight.
   It is important to press the
'sausages' firmly on to the
skewers to prevent them falling
off during cooking.
   Do not overcook the kebabs
or they will be hard and dry.

●270 calories/1125 kj per portion

Pork and aubergine kebabs

SERVES 4

750 g/1½ lb boneless pork, trimmed of excess fat and cut into 2.5 cm/ 1 inch cubes (see Buying guide)
1 small aubergine, cut into 1 cm/ ½ inch slices
salt
2 small onions, cut into quarters
8 bay leaves
vegetable oil, for greasing
lemon wedges, to garnish

MARINADE

150 ml/¼ pint vegetable oil (see Cook's tip)
juice of 1 lemon
2 teaspoons dried oregano
freshly ground black pepper

1 Cut the aubergine slices into thirds, place in a colander and sprinkle with salt. Weight down and leave for 20 minutes to extract the excess juices, then rinse slices and pat dry on absorbent paper.

2 Combine all the marinade ingredients in a large bowl, adding salt and pepper to taste. Add the cubed pork and aubergine and turn to coat thoroughly. Cover the dish with cling film and leave to marinate in the refrigerator for at least 3 hours or overnight, turning the ingredients in the marinade once or twice during this time.

3 Light the barbecue.

4 Brush 4 long kebab skewers with oil. Transfer the pork and aubergine pieces from the marinade to a plate, reserving the excess marinade. Separate each onion quarter into 2 layers (see Preparation).

5 Thread the pork, aubergine, onion pieces and the bay leaves on to the 4 oiled skewers, alternating the ingredients.

6 When the coals are hot, brush kebabs with the reserved marinade and place on the grid. Cook the kebabs for 12-15 minutes until cooked through, turning several times and brushing with the reserved marinade.

7 Transfer the cooked kebabs to individual dinner plates, spear a lemon wedge on to each skewer and serve at once.

Cook's Notes

TIME
Preliminary preparation, including preparing the aubergine, takes about 25 minutes. Allow at least 3 hours marinating time. Assembling and cooking the kebabs then takes about 30 minutes.

COOK'S TIP
Olive oil gives the kebabs the best flavour, but ordinary vegetable oil can be used instead.

PREPARATION
To prepare onions for kebabs:

Carefully separate each onion quarter into 2 layers.

BUYING GUIDE
Pork steaks, available packaged from supermarkets, are a good buy for this recipe. Choose thick steaks.

SERVING IDEAS
Serve the kebabs with short-cut wholemeal macaroni as a change from rice, and a salad of shredded lettuce and sliced tomatoes.

● 435 calories/1825 kj per portion

Skewered pork 'n' kidney

SERVES 4

250 g/9 oz lean pork, cut into
    2.5 cm/1 inch cubes
250 g/9 oz lamb kidneys, halved
4 streaky bacon rashers, rinds
    removed, cut into 2.5 cm/1 inch
    squares
2 dessert apples, cored and
    quartered
12 bay leaves
2 teaspoons French mustard
salt and freshly ground black pepper
vegetable oil, for brushing
parsley sprigs and lemon wedges,
    to garnish (optional)

1 Light the barbecue. Brush 4 kebab skewers with oil.
2 Thread the pork, bacon, kidney halves, apple quarters and bay leaves on to the skewers, alternating the ingredients.
3 Brush the pork and kidney pieces with mustard. Brush all the ingredients with oil and season lightly with salt and pepper.
4 When the coals are hot, cook kebabs for 12-15 minutes turning often, ⚠ and brushing with more oil, to keep the meat moist.
5 Arrange the cooked kebabs on a serving dish and serve at once, garnished with parsley sprigs and lemon wedges, if liked.

Cook's Notes

TIME
Preparation and cooking take about 30 minutes.

⚠ WATCHPOINT
When barbecuing the kebabs, ensure that the skewers are turned often so that all the different ingredients are thoroughly cooked.

SERVING IDEAS
Serve the kebabs with boiled rice (allow 50 g/ 2 oz uncooked weight per person) and a green salad with an oil and vinegar dressing.

●210 calories/875 kj per portion

Sausage and bacon kebabs

SERVES 4
8 pork chipolata sausages
8 streaky bacon rashers, rinds removed
1 small green pepper, deseeded, and cut into 2.5 cm/1 inch pieces
8 small onions
4 small tomatoes, halved
12 button mushrooms, trimmed
50 g/2 oz margarine or butter, softened
1 tablespoon French mustard
dash of Worcestershire sauce
vegetable oil, for greasing

1 Light the barbecue. Brush 4 kebab skewers with oil.
2 Twist each sausage in 2 places and cut into 3 tiny sausages, making 24 in all.
3 Thread the sausages, bacon and vegetables on to the oiled skewers, alternating the ingredients: start with a tomato half, then thread on a bacon rasher and weave it round the other ingredients as you thread them on (see Preparation). Finish each kebab with a tomato half.
4 Cream the margarine with mustard and Worcestershire sauce and brush the mixture over the kebabs.
5 When the coals are hot, place the kebabs on the grid and cook for about 7-10 minutes, turning occasionally, until the sausages are cooked through.
6 Remove the kebabs from the barbecue and serve at once.

Cook's Notes

 TIME
Preparation takes 20-25 minutes, cooking 7-10 minutes.

 SERVING IDEAS
Remove skewers and serve kebabs in wholemeal pitta bread or on a bed of rice flavoured with chopped fresh herbs.

 VARIATIONS
Pieces of frankfurter or garlic sausage can be substituted for the chipolatas.

 PREPARATION
To thread meat and vegetables on to the skewers:

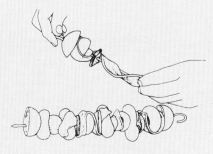

●485 calories/2025 kj per portion

Skewered lamb with apricots

SERVES 4

500 g/1 lb boneless lamb, trimmed of excess fat and cut into 2.5 cm/1 inch cubes (see Buying guide)
400 g/14 oz can apricot halves, drained with 4 tablespoons syrup reserved
1 large green pepper, cubed
1 small aubergine, cubed
16 bay leaves
vegetable oil, for greasing

MARINADE

2 tablespoons vegetable oil
1 tablespoon white wine vinegar
1 clove garlic, crushed (optional)
1 onion, chopped
½ teaspoon dried thyme
1 teaspoon soy sauce
salt and freshly ground black pepper

SAUCE

15 g/½ oz margarine or butter
1 onion, chopped
1 clove garlic, crushed (optional)
1 tablespoon white wine vinegar
1 teaspoon French mustard
150 ml/¼ pint water
dash of Tabasco
1 tablespoon tomato purée

1 Combine all the marinade ingredients in a saucepan with 2 tablespoons of the reserved canned apricot syrup and bring to the boil. Lower heat and simmer for 3-4 minutes, then leave to cool.
2 Put the lamb cubes into a bowl, pour over the marinade, cover and leave to marinate in the refrigerator for 2 hours, stirring from time to time.
3 Light the barbecue. Brush 4 kebab skewers with oil.
4 About 20 minutes before coals are ready for cooking, prepare the sauce: melt the margarine in a frying-pan, add the onion and garlic, if using, and fry over moderate heat for 2 minutes. Stir in the vinegar, mustard, water, Tabasco, tomato purée and 2 tablespoons of the reserved canned apricot syrup. Lower the heat and simmer for 15 minutes. Remove from the heat and cover the surface of the sauce closely with cling film.
5 Thread the cubes of lamb on to the oiled skewers, alternating with apricot halves, green pepper, aubergine and bay leaves. Reserve the marinade.
6 When the coals are hot, brush the kebabs with the reserved marinade and place on the grid. Cook over the coals for about 10 minutes, turning the skewers and basting the lamb with the marinade from time to time.
7 Meanwhile, uncover the sauce and reheat gently, stirring vigorously. Serve the lamb on the skewers at once, with the reheated sauce handed separately in a warmed jug.

Cook's Notes

 TIME
Preparation takes about 30 minutes. Allow 2 hours for marinating. Cooking takes about 10 minutes.

WATCHPOINT
Do not overcook the kebabs or they will lose their moistness.

BUYING GUIDE
Buy best lean lamb, ideally from the leg.

 SERVING IDEAS
Serve on a bed of rice and accompany with a mixed salad.

●300 calories/1250 kj per portion

Indian skewered lamb

SERVES 4

750 g/1½ lb boneless lamb,
  trimmed of excess fat and cut
  into 2.5 cm/1 inch cubes (see
  Buying guide)
300 g/10 oz natural yoghurt
1 onion, finely grated
1 teaspoon ground ginger
2 tablespoons garam masala (see
  Buying guide)
½ teaspoon chilli powder
salt
1 green pepper, deseeded and
  cut into 2.5 cm/1 inch squares
1 red pepper, deseeded and
  cut into 2.5 cm/1 inch squares
12 button mushrooms, trimmed
vegetable oil, for brushing

1 In a large bowl, mix together the
yoghurt, onion, ginger, garam
masala, chilli powder and salt to
taste. Add the cubes of lamb to the
mixture, turning them over so that
each piece is well-coated. Cover with
cling film and leave to marinate in a
cool place (not in the refrigerator)
overnight.

2 Light the barbecue. Brush 4 kebab
skewers with oil.

3 Remove the lamb from the
marinade but do not wipe off the
yoghurt coating. Thread the meat,
the green and red peppers and
mushrooms in turn on to the oiled
kebab skewers.

4 When the coals are hot, brush
the lamb kebabs all over with oil.
Place the kebabs on the grid and
cook over the hot coals for about 10
minutes, turning the skewers frequently, so that the ingredients
cook evenly. Brush the kebabs with
more oil from time to time to keep
the meat moist.

5 Transfer the lamb kebabs to a
serving dish or individual dinner
plates and serve at once.

Vegetable kebabs

SERVES 4

3 small courgettes, cut into
   4 cm/1½ inch slices
12 whole button onions
salt
12 whole button mushrooms
8 tomatoes, halved
8 small bay leaves
50 g/2 oz margarine or butter,
   melted
vegetable oil, for greasing

MARINADE
6 tablespoons vegetable oil
1 tablespoon lemon juice
1 small onion, finely chopped
2 tablespoons chopped fresh
   parsley
1 clove garlic, crushed (optional)
salt and freshly ground black pepper

1 Bring a saucepan of salted water
to the boil, add the courgette slices
and button onions and boil gently
for 1 minute. Drain and immediately plunge the vegetables into
cold water to prevent them cooking
further. Drain vegetables well again
and pat dry with absorbent paper.
2 Divide the courgette slices,
onions, mushrooms, tomatoes and
bay leaves into 4 equal
portions and

thread them on to 4 greased metal
kebab skewers, alternating the
shapes and colours as much as
possible. Lay the skewers in a
shallow dish.
3 To make the marinade: put all the
ingredients in a screw-top jar with
salt and pepper to taste. Shake well
to mix. Pour the marinade over the
vegetable kebabs and leave them in
a cool place for about 2 hours,
turning them occasionally to coat
the vegetables evenly.
4 Light the barbecue.
5 When the coals are hot, lift
kebabs from the marinade and allow

any excess dressing to drain off.
Brush the vegetables with the
melted margarine. Place on the grid
and cook for about 8 minutes, turning frequently to brown the vegetables evenly. Serve at once.

Cook's Notes

TIME
2¾ hours in total,
including marinating.

SERVING IDEAS
Serve on a bed of herb-
flavoured rice.

● 230 calories/975 kj per portion

Spicy vegetable kebabs

SERVES 6

1 green and 1 red pepper, each deseeded and cut into about 12 squares
12 button onions
salt
12 button mushrooms
500 g/1 lb can pineapple cubes, drained
vegetable oil, for greasing

SAUCE

2 × 150 g/5 oz cartons natural yoghurt
2 cloves garlic, crushed
5 cm/2 inch piece of fresh root ginger, peeled and grated
2 teaspoons garam masala
juice of 1 lemon
pinch of salt

1 Light the barbecue. Brush 6 kebab skewers with oil.

2 Make the sauce: put all the sauce ingredients in a bowl, mix well and leave to stand for 30 minutes to allow the flavours to blend.

3 Meanwhile, blanch the peppers and onions: bring a large pan of salted water to the boil, add the peppers and onions and boil for 1 minute. Drain and immediately plunge into cold water to prevent further cooking. Drain well again and pat dry with absorbent paper.

4 Divide the peppers, onions, mushrooms and pineapple pieces into 6 portions and thread them on to the oiled metal kebab skewers, alternating the shapes and colours.

5 When the coals are hot, brush the kebabs with some of the sauce and place on the grid. Cook for 8 minutes, turning them every few minutes and brushing with more sauce, until vegetables are evenly browned. Serve at once.

Cook's Notes

TIME
1 hour to prepare and cook the spicy vegetable kebabs from start to finish.

SERVING IDEAS
These kebabs make an excellent vegetarian dish, served with lightly spiced brown or white rice.

Alternatively, the spicy flavour of the vegetables makes the kebabs a good partner to plainly-barbecued lamb chops, burgers or sausages.

VARIATION
Try adding bacon rolls to each skewer for more substantial kebabs. Use three bacon rolls per skewer.

●100 calories/425 kj per portion

Herby fish kebabs

SERVES 4
750 g/1½ lb boneless cod steaks, skinned
2 tablespoons lemon juice
1 tablespoon vegetable oil
1 teaspoon Worcestershire sauce
1 tablespoon chopped mixed fresh herbs, or 1 teaspoon dried basil
good pinch of fresh chopped dill or dried chopped dillweed
salt and freshly ground black pepper
1 large green pepper, deseeded
4 small tomatoes, halved
vegetable oil, for greasing

1 Light the barbecue. Brush 8 small kebab skewers with oil.
2 Cut the fish into 32 cubes and place on a large plate. In a bowl mix together the lemon juice, oil, Worcestershire sauce and herbs. Season well with salt and pepper and pour over the fish. Leave to stand for 5 minutes, turning the cubes of fish in the marinade from time to time.
3 Put the green pepper in a bowl and cover with boiling water. Leave to stand for 5 minutes. Drain well, then cut into chunky pieces big enough to thread on to skewers.
4 Slide alternate pieces of fish and green pepper on to the skewers. Complete each skewer with a halved tomato. Reserve the marinade.
5 When the coals are hot, place the kebabs on the grid and cook for about 8 minutes, turning as necessary and brushing with the reserved marinade [!] until the fish is cooked. Serve at once.

Cook's Notes

 TIME
Preparation 15 minutes, cooking 8 minutes.

 WATCHPOINT
The basting is necessary to avoid the fish becoming dry during cooking.

 SERVING IDEAS
For an unusual potato accompaniment to serve with these, prepare 4 portions of creamed potato and spread evenly over a shallow heatproof serving dish. Sprinkle with a little grated cheese and place under a hot grill until golden. Arrange the fish kebabs on top of the browned potato and garnish with lemon slices and watercress. Serve with mayonnaise or tartare sauce handed separately in a small bowl.

Alternatively, serve the herby fish kebabs on a fresh-looking bed of shredded lettuce or roughly chopped watercress.

 VARIATIONS
Use raw cucumber instead of blanched green pepper. Add 1 tablespoon dry vermouth to the marinade.

●180 calories/750 kj per portion

Seafood and orange kebabs

SERVES 4
500 g/1 lb fish fillet, skinned and cut into 2.5 cm/1 inch cubes
250 g/8 oz unpeeled prawns
3 large oranges
vegetable oil, for greasing

MARINADE
4 tablespoons vegetable oil
4 tablespoons lemon juice
½ teaspoon dried marjoram
1 large clove garlic, crushed (optional)
salt and freshly ground black pepper

1 Light the barbecue. Brush 4 kebab skewers with oil.
2 Combine all the marinade ingredients in a large shallow dish. Then, add the fish cubes and prawns and turn to coat (see Cook's tip). Leave fish and prawns to marinate for 30 minutes at room temperature.
3 Meanwhile, peel and segment the oranges over the marinade, so that any juice drips into it. Set the orange segments aside on a plate
4 Remove all the fish cubes and prawns from the marinade and thread them and the orange segments on to the oiled kebab skewers (see Preparation).

5 When the coals are hot, brush the kebabs with some of the marinade and place on the barbecue grid. Cook for about 8 minutes, turning once and brushing occasionally with more marinade. [!]
6 Arrange the cooked kebabs on a warmed large serving plate. Brush the kebabs with the remaining marinade and serve at once.

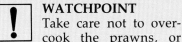

Cook's Notes

 TIME
Preparation takes 20-25 minutes. Allow 30 minutes for marinating. Cooking the kebabs takes about 8 minutes.

 PREPARATION
When threading the prawns on to the kebab skewers, push the skewer through the thickest part of the body so that they do not fall off during cooking.

COOK'S TIP
If you prefer not to peel the prawns after cooking, use peeled jumbo prawns on the kebabs instead.

[!] WATCHPOINT
Take care not to overcook the prawns, or they will become hard and tough. Raise the grid if they begin to brown too quickly.

●270 calories/1125 kj per portion

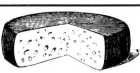

Chilli sausage burgers

SERVES 4-6
500 g/1 lb pork sausagemeat
1 onion, grated
1 large carrot, grated
50 g/2 oz fresh white breadcrumbs
4 tablespoons tomato ketchup
1 tablespoon chilli seasoning (see Did you know)
¼ teaspoon ground mixed spice
salt and freshly ground black pepper
vegetable oil, for greasing

1 Light the barbecue.
2 Combine all the ingredients (except the oil) in a large bowl, using floured fingertips to mix well. Season with salt and pepper.
3 With floured hands, !️ divide the mixture into 4-6 portions and roll them into balls. Flatten each slightly. Chill the burgers in the refrigerator for 30 minutes, then leave at room temperature for a few minutes before you start cooking (see Cook's tip).

4 When the coals are hot, brush the grid with oil. Place the burgers on the grid and cook for about 10 minutes, turning once, until browned and cooked through. Serve at once.

Cook's Notes

 TIME
Preparation 15 minutes, plus chilling, then about 10 minutes cooking.

 COOK'S TIP
Chilling the burgers before cooking improves their flavour and texture.

⚠ WATCHPOINT
The sausagemeat mixture is very sticky, so flour your hands well before shaping the burgers.

 SERVING IDEAS
Serve the burgers with French fries and a salad, or in soft baps like hamburgers.

 DID YOU KNOW
Chilli seasoning is one of the hottest flavourings for food (although not as hot as real chilli powder). It is a mixture of garlic, dried powdered chilli pepper and herbs and spices such as oregano and cumin.

● 570 calories/2400 kj per portion

20

Surprise hamburgers

SERVES 4
750 g/1½ lb lean minced beef
1 small onion, finely grated
1 tablespoon tomato ketchup
salt and freshly ground black pepper
75 g/3 oz Danish Blue cheese,
  mashed
vegetable oil, for greasing

1 In a large bowl, mix together the minced beef, onion and tomato ketchup and season well with salt and pepper. ✳ Cover the mixture and refrigerate for 1 hour.
2 Light the barbecue.
3 Divide the mashed cheese into 4 portions. Shape each portion into a ball and flatten slightly. Divide the chilled beef mixture into 4 portions and mould 1 portion around each ball of cheese. Shape into a fairly thick hamburger, making sure that the cheese is completely enclosed by the meat mixture.
4 When the coals are hot, brush the grid with oil. Place hamburgers on the grid and cook for about 15 minutes, turning once, until they are browned and cooked through. Transfer to a serving dish and serve at once.

Cook's Notes

TIME
Preparation takes 10 minutes but allow 1 hour chilling time. Cooking then takes about 15 minutes.

FREEZING
Shape beef mixture round the cheese as in stage 3. Open freeze hamburgers until solid, then wrap individually in foil and pack together in a polythene bag. Seal, label and return to the freezer for up to 3 months. To serve: defrost at room temperature, light the barbecue, then proceed from stage 4.

VARIATIONS
Grated mature Cheddar cheese or finely shredded Mozzarella may be substituted for the Danish Blue.
Add a few drops of Tabasco to the minced beef mixture, for a more piquant taste.

SERVING IDEAS
Serve in the traditional sesame bun with lettuce, sliced tomato and various relishes or mustard. Alternatively, serve with French fried potatoes, without the bun.

●415 calories/1750 kj per portion

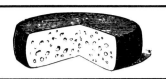

Devilled lamb

SERVES 4-6

1.5 kg/3-3½ lb shoulder of lamb
2 tablespoons plain flour
salt and freshly ground black pepper
1 tablespoon French mustard
¾ teaspoon sweet paprika
about ¼ teaspoon cayenne pepper
50 g/2 oz butter, softened
2 teaspoons lemon juice

1 Light the barbecue.

2 Season the flour with salt and pepper, then rub all over the lamb. Reserve any excess flour.
3 When the coals are hot, put the lamb on a rotisserie and cook for 40 minutes.
4 Meanwhile, make the devilled mixture: blend the mustard, paprika, cayenne and ¼ teaspoon salt with the butter. Stir in lemon juice.
5 Make six 1 cm/½ inch deep slashes in the skin side of the lamb. Spread half devilled mixture in the slashes; spread rest over surface of meat. Sprinkle with seasoned flour.
6 Cook the lamb for a further 30-40 minutes until cooked. Serve at once.

Cook's Notes

TIME
Preparation and cooking take about 1½ hours.

SERVING IDEAS
This adventurous lamb dish is delicious served with a crisp salad, made up of lettuce, onion rings and sliced cucumber and radishes.

Hot garlic bread is another good accompaniment.

●805 calories/3390 kj per portion

Pineapple barbecued steak

SERVES 4

4 pieces best braising steak, each
    weighing 175-225 g/6-8 oz, cut
    about 2 cm/¾ inch thick
25 g/1 oz margarine or butter
1 small onion, finely chopped
225 ml/8 fl oz tomato ketchup
4 tablespoons lemon juice
2 tablespoons red wine vinegar
1 tablespoon Worcestershire sauce
2 tablespoons light soft brown
    sugar
1 teaspoon mustard powder
salt and freshly ground black pepper
150 ml/¼ pint natural pineapple
    juice (see Buying guide)

1 Melt the margarine in a saucepan, add the onion and fry gently for 5 minutes until soft and lightly coloured.
2 Stir in the tomato ketchup, lemon juice, vinegar, Worcestershire sauce, sugar, mustard and salt and pepper to taste. Bring to the boil, then lower the heat, cover and simmer gently for 20 minutes, stirring occasionally.
3 Remove the pan from the heat and stir in the pineapple juice.
4 Arrange the pieces of steak, in 1 layer, in a shallow dish. Pour over the barbecue sauce. Cover and leave to marinate in the refrigerator overnight.
5 Light the barbecue.
6 When the coals are hot, lift the steaks out of the marinade with kitchen tongs and place them on the grid. Reserve the marinade. Cook the steaks for about 5 minutes on each side, until they are cooked to your liking.
7 Meanwhile, pour the marinade into a saucepan and heat through gently on top of the grid. Brush the sauce over the steaks from time to time while they are cooking, and serve them with the remaining sauce.

Barbecued chicken drumsticks

SERVES 4
8 chicken drumsticks
4 tablespoons tomato ketchup
2 tablespoons Worcestershire sauce
½ small onion, finely chopped
25 g/1 oz soft brown sugar
1 tablespoon lemon juice
celery salt
sweet paprika

1 Combine the tomato ketchup with the Worcestershire sauce, onion, sugar and lemon juice. Season with celery salt and paprika to taste. Brush the mixture over the drumsticks. Leave to marinate in a cool place for as long as possible (up to 8 hours, see Cook's tips).
2 Light the barbecue.

3 When the coals are hot, remove the drumsticks from the marinade with kitchen tongs and place on the grid. Reserve the marinade. Cook the drumsticks for 15-20 minutes until cooked through, turning and brushing occasionally with the reserved marinade. Serve at once.

Cook's Notes

TIME
Preparation 5 minutes, and up to 8 hours to marinate. Cooking takes 15-20 minutes.

SERVING IDEAS
Serve with sautéed sliced aubergines, green or red peppers and tomatoes, accompanied by chopped cucumber with yoghurt and crusty bread.

VARIATIONS
Chinese-style spare ribs of pork can be cooked in the same way; so, too, can strips of belly pork.

COOK'S TIPS
The flavour is improved if the drumsticks are left to marinate for several hours. The drumsticks can be skinned before marinating if preferred, but the skin does help keep the flesh moist during cooking. To test if a drumstick is cooked, pierce the thickest part with a skewer — the juice should run clear.

●275 calories/1150 kj per portion

Apricot barbecue chicken

SERVES 4-6
12 chicken drumsticks (see Cook's tip)
toasted almonds, to garnish (optional)
vegetable oil, for greasing

BARBECUE SAUCE
400 g/14 oz can apricots
2 tablespoons malt vinegar
2 tablespoons light soy sauce
1 clove garlic, crushed (optional)
2.5 cm/1 inch piece fresh root ginger, peeled and crushed
pinch of dried tarragon (optional)
salt and freshly ground black pepper

1 Light the barbecue.
2 Make the sauce: put the apricots and their syrup into the goblet of a blender, add the remaining sauce ingredients with salt and pepper to taste and work for a few seconds to a rough purée.
3 Turn the apricot mixture into a saucepan and bring to the boil. Boil, stirring, for 2-3 minutes until it thickens to a coating consistency.
4 When the coals are hot, brush the grid with oil, then place the drumsticks on the oiled grid. Brush the drumsticks thickly with half the sauce. Cook them for 15-20 minutes until the juices run clear when the thickest part of the drumsticks is pierced with a fine skewer. Turn the drumsticks over once or twice during cooking time and brush with the remaining barbecue sauce from time to time.
5 Transfer drumsticks to a serving platter and spoon over any leftover barbecue sauce, then sprinkle with the toasted almonds, if using, and serve at once.

Cook's Notes

TIME
Preparing and cooking take about 40 minutes.

VARIATIONS
Use 350 g/12 oz fresh ripe apricots instead of canned. Simmer the peeled, halved and stoned apricots with 300 ml/½ pint water and 75 g/3 oz sugar for 10-15 minutes then follow the recipe.

Use sauce to baste chicken wings and cook them on a barbecue to make tasty finger food.

COOK'S TIP
The chicken can be skinned before cooking if preferred, but bear in mind that the skin helps keep the flesh moist during cooking.

●300 calories/1250 kj per portion

Spicy lamb chops

SERVES 4

12 breakfast or thin-cut lamb
   chops, each weighing about
   25-50 g/1-2 oz, defrosted
   if frozen
juice of 1 lemon
1 teaspoon salt
1 clove garlic, crushed (optional)
1 onion, finely chopped
1 teaspoon ground coriander
½ teaspoon ground ginger
¼ teaspoon chilli powder or
   seasoning
¼ teaspoon sweet paprika
150 g/5 oz natural yoghurt
lime or lemon wedges and extra
   sweet paprika, to garnish

1 Put the chops on a board then, using a small sharp knife, make several slits in each. Sprinkle the chops with a little of the lemon juice and all the salt.
2 Mix the remaining lemon juice with the garlic, if using, the onion, coriander, ginger, chilli powder, paprika and yoghurt.
3 Arrange the chops in a single layer in a shallow dish and spread with half the yoghurt mixture. Turn the chops over and coat with the remaining yoghurt mixture. Cover and leave to marinate for at least 4 hours in a cool place.
4 Light the barbecue.
5 When the coals are hot, lift chops from the dish and place on the grid. Cook for 4 minutes on each side until cooked through. Serve at once with lime wedges.

Cook's Notes

TIME
Preparation 15 minutes; marinating 4 hours or overnight; cooking 8 minutes.

SERVING IDEAS
These tasty chops can be eaten with the fingers.

VARIATION
Use skinned chicken drumsticks instead of lamb chops. Depending on the size they will take 15-20 minutes to cook.

●240 calories/1000 kj per portion

Zorba chicken

SERVES 4
1.5 kg/3-3½ lb oven-ready chicken,
 thoroughly defrosted if frozen,
 divided into quarters
2 tablespoons olive oil
1 clove garlic, crushed
2 tablespoons chopped fresh
 thyme, or 2 teaspoons dried
 thyme
salt and freshly ground black pepper

1 Light the barbecue.
2 Pat the chicken dry with absorbent
paper. Cut 4 double thickness
squares of foil each large enough to
contain a chicken piece.

Cook's Notes

TIME
Preparation takes about
15 minutes, cooking
about 45 minutes.

DID YOU KNOW
This simple way of cook-
ing chicken is a very
popular taverna dish in Greece.

●605 calories/2525 kj per portion

SERVING IDEAS
Serve with hot pitta
bread and a Greek-style
salad of sliced tomatoes, cucumber, spring onions and shredded
cabbage, garnished with black
olives and slices of Feta cheese,
if liked.
 A glass of well-chilled retsina
wine is a good accompaniment
for the foil-cooked chicken.

3 Heat the oil in a large frying-pan,
add the chicken pieces and fry quickly to brown on all sides.
4 Put a chicken piece on each foil
square, skin side up. Brush chicken
pieces all over with the oil remaining in the pan, then sprinkle with

the garlic and thyme. Season well.
Seal the foil edges together tightly,
to make parcels.
5 When the coals are hot, place the
chicken parcels on the grid and cook
for about 45 minutes until cooked
through. Serve at once in the foil.

Trout with golden sauce

SERVES 4

4 rainbow trout, each weighing about 350 g/12 oz, cleaned with heads and tails left on (see Buying guide)
1 tablespoon vegetable oil
salt and freshly ground black pepper
2 tablespoons thick bottled mayonnaise
1 tablespoon French mustard
2 teaspoons finely chopped fresh parsley or tarragon or 1 teaspoon dried dillweed
1 teaspoon lemon juice
vegetable oil, for greasing
lemon wedges, to serve

1 Light the barbecue.
2 Pat the trout dry with absorbent paper. Brush them all over with oil, and then sprinkle with salt and freshly ground black pepper.
3 Mix the mayonnaise, mustard, parsley and lemon juice together in a bowl.
4 When the coals are hot, brush the grid with oil, place the trout on grid and cook for about 10 minutes, turning once, until fish flakes easily. Remove from grid.
5 Spread the mustard sauce evenly over the trout, place on the grid and barbecue them for a further 2 minutes, until the skin of the trout starts to split and the sauce is golden brown. Transfer the trout to a warmed serving dish and serve at once, with lemon wedges handed separately.

Cook's Notes

TIME
Preparation takes about 10 minutes, cooking about 12 minutes.

COOK'S TIP
Make slashes in the thicker parts of the fish, to help even cooking.

SERVING IDEAS
Serve with hot herbed bread in foil.

BUYING GUIDE
Defrosted frozen trout can be used.

● 430 calories/1800 kj per portion

Mackerel with horseradish

SERVES 4

4 mackerel, each weighing about 350 g/12 oz, slit and cleaned
150 ml/¼ pint double cream
2 teaspoons grated horseradish (see Buying guide)
½ teaspoon made English mustard
6 spring onions, finely chopped
salt and freshly ground black pepper
margarine, for greasing
lemon wedges, to serve

1 Light the barbecue.
2 Cut 4 pieces of foil large enough to enclose each mackerel completely. Grease the foil. Place each mackerel on a piece of foil.
3 In a bowl, mix all the remaining ingredients well together and spoon a quarter of the mixture into the middle of each mackerel. Reshape the fish.
4 Fold over the edges of the foil, crimping them tightly together to make sure the steam cannot escape from the parcels. !
5 When the coals are hot, place the parcels on the grid and cook for 30 minutes, until the fish flakes easily with a knife.
6 Serve at once in foil, with lemon wedges handed separately.

Cook's Notes

TIME
Preparation and cooking take about 40 minutes.

BUYING GUIDE
The yellowish-white, pungently flavoured horseradish root is not always easy to obtain, but is most likely to be found in Asian food shops and street markets. Fresh horseradish has a wonderfully hot taste and it is well worth trying: scrub the root well, remove any tubers and discoloured bits, then grate the outer part, which has the strongest flavour, and discard the core. A jar of ready-grated horseradish can be used for this recipe, but do not buy bottled horseradish sauce or the creamed variety as neither are suitable here.

! WATCHPOINT
As the stuffing may be a little runny, the foil parcels must be really tightly sealed to prevent any of it running out.

● 600 calories/2500 kj per portion

Barbecue treats

MAKES 8
1 small French loaf
50 g/2 oz butter
2 teaspoons French mustard
1 tablespoon chopped fresh parsley
250 g/9 oz cooked chicken, sliced
100 g/4 oz Stilton cheese, grated
2 tomatoes, sliced
8 stuffed olives, sliced

1 Heat the oven to 200C/400F/Gas 6.
2 Cut the loaf into 4 pieces, then slice each piece in half horizontally.
3 Beat the butter, mustard and parsley together until smooth, then spread on the bread. Arrange the chicken slices on top.
4 Sprinkle over the grated cheese and arrange the tomato and stuffed olive slices on top.
5 Wrap the bread slices individually or side-by-side in pairs in foil (see Cook's tip) and place the parcels on a baking sheet.
6 Bake in the oven for 20-25 minutes until the grated Stilton cheese has melted.
7 Unwrap the parcels, transfer to a warmed serving plate and serve at once.

Cook's Notes

 TIME
10 minutes to prepare, plus 20-25 minutes cooking time.

 VARIATIONS
Thinly sliced Dolcelatte cheese can be used instead of Stilton. Use cold roast pork or beef instead of chicken.

 COOK'S TIP
If a crusty finish is preferred, do not wrap slices in foil, just place on the baking sheet and bake in the oven for 10 minutes.

 SERVING IDEAS
Serve still wrapped in the foil for a barbecue. These parcels can also be served cold on a picnic. Bake in the oven, allow to cool, then pack in the picnic basket still in their foil parcels.

● 225 calories/925 kj per slice

Spicy relish

SERVES 4-6
500 g/1 lb tomatoes, skinned and
  chopped
2 onions, finely chopped
1 clove garlic, chopped (optional)
50 g/2 oz dark Barbados sugar (see
  Did you know)
3 tablespoons Worcestershire
  sauce
2 tablespoons soy sauce
2 tablespoons malt vinegar

1 Put the tomatoes and onions into a saucepan with all the remaining ingredients. Bring slowly to the boil, then lower the heat and simmer, uncovered, for 45 minutes until very thick—the finished relish should measure about 300 ml/½ pint. !

2 Transfer to a small bowl and serve hot, or cool completely before serving.

Cook's Notes

 TIME
The relish will take about 15 minutes to prepare and 45 minutes to cook.

 DID YOU KNOW
Barbados sugar is sometimes called raw sugar. It is less refined than white sugar and contains small amounts of natural vitamins and minerals. Large supermarkets and health food shops usually stock it, in light and dark brown varieties.

 SERVING IDEAS
Served cold from a relish tray, this relish is very good with hamburgers. It can also be served hot with barbecued steaks, chicken pieces, chops and sausages.

! **WATCHPOINT**
Stir towards the end of the cooking time to make sure the relish does not stick to the bottom of the pan.

● 100 calories/425 kj per portion

PARTIES

Barbecue dinner

On a fine summer's evening, what could be more enjoyable than a relaxed barbecue dinner with friends. Cooking in the open is a lot of fun and so easy to organise — less washing up for you and guests can join in with the cooking! This menu starts with an easy-to-make soup, follows with tasty beef kebabs and tangy sauce, and rounds off with a delicious strawberry flan, plus an unusual idea for a cheeseboard.

Creamy watercress soup

SERVES 4
2 bunches watercress
1 onion, quartered
600 ml/1 pint well-flavoured
   chicken stock (see Economy)
1 teaspoon lemon juice
salt and freshly ground black pepper
25 g/1 oz cornflour
300 ml/½ pint milk
pinch of freshly grated nutmeg

Cook's Notes

Creamy watercress Soup

TIME
This soup takes 45 minutes to make.

VARIATION
Substitute 250 g/9 oz frozen leaf or chopped spinach for the watercress.

ECONOMY
To be even more econo-mical, and improve the flavour, make your own stock from a left-over chicken carcass.

COOK'S TIP
A quick way to blend the cornflour and milk without first making a paste is to whizz it for a few seconds in blender, after puréeing soup.

●95 calories/400 kj per portion

1 Put watercress into a saucepan, reserving a few sprigs for the garnish. Add the onion, chicken stock, lemon juice and salt and pepper to taste.
2 Bring to the boil, then lower the heat, cover the pan and simmer for 30 minutes, stirring occasionally. Remove the pan from the heat and leave the soup to cool slightly.
3 Work the soup to a smooth purée in a blender or press the soup through a sieve.
4 Return the soup to the rinsed-out pan. Mix the cornflour to a paste with a little of the milk, then stir in the remaining milk. Stir this mixture slowly into the soup, then bring to the boil, stirring all the time. Simmer for 2 minutes.
5 Add the nutmeg, taste and adjust seasoning, then pour into warmed individual soup bowls. Serve hot, garnished with watercress.

Beefball and apricot kebabs

SERVES 4
500 g/1 lb lean minced beef
1 small onion, grated
25 g/1 oz fresh white breadcrumbs
½ teaspoon ground ginger
¼ teaspoon dried thyme
½ teaspoon salt
¼ teaspoon freshly ground black
   pepper
1 egg, lightly beaten
6 rashers streaky bacon, rinds
   removed
6 large dried apricots, halved
vegetable oil, for greasing

1 Light the barbecue. Brush 4 kebab skewers with oil.
2 Mix together the beef, onion, breadcrumbs, ginger, thyme and salt and pepper. Add the egg, then mix with your hands until combined (see Cook's tip). Shape into 16 balls.
3 Cut each bacon rasher in half, then wrap around each apricot half.
4 Thread the meatballs and apricots in bacon alternately on to skewers, allowing 4 meatballs and 3 apricots in bacon for each. ✳
5 When the coals are hot, place the kebabs on the grid and cook for about 10 minutes, turning frequently, until they are browned and cooked through. ⚠ Serve at once on a bed of boiled rice.

Barbecue sauce

SERVES 4
3 tablespoons wine vinegar
2 tablespoons dark soft brown sugar
2 tablespoons tomato ketchup
2 tablespoons fruit chutney
2 teaspoons cornflour
2 teaspoons soy sauce
300 ml/½ pint water
salt and freshly ground black pepper

1 Make the sauce: put all the in-gredients in a saucepan and bring to the boil, stirring constantly. Boil the sauce for 2 minutes.
2 Transfer the sauce to a small bowl and serve at once, while still hot, with the kebabs.

Cook's Notes

Beefball and apricot kebabs

TIME
The kebabs take 35 minutes.

COOK'S TIP
Mixing the meat with your hands is quick, and makes it easier to shape.

BUYING GUIDE
Make sure you buy really lean minced beef for this dish. Fatty minced beef will make the meatballs shrink and lose their shape when cooked, so it is a false economy.

WATCHPOINT
If the kebabs look as if they are going to burn raise the grid and continue to barbecue until they are cooked through.

FREEZING
Wrap the uncooked kebabs individually in foil or cling film. Place in a polythene bag, seal, label and freeze for up to 2 months. To serve: unwrap the kebabs and cook from frozen for about 15 minutes until cooked through.

Barbecue sauce

TIME
The sauce takes about 5 minutes.

●525 calories/2200 kj per kebab with portion of sauce

Strawberry flan

SERVES 4
500 g/1 lb fresh strawberries, hulled and halved lengthways
40 g/1½ oz unsalted pistachio nuts, split in half
225 g/8 oz strawberry jam
3 tablespoons water
2 teaspoons powdered gelatine
1 egg white
300 ml/½ pint double cream
1 tablespoon caster sugar
1 teaspoon vanilla flavouring

PASTRY
225 g/8 oz plain flour
pinch of salt
2 teaspoons caster sugar
175 g/6 oz butter, diced
1 egg yolk
1 tablespoon cold water

1 Make the pastry: sift the flour and salt into a bowl and stir in the sugar. Make a well in the centre and add the butter, egg yolk and water. Gradually work the dry ingredients into the centre until the dough forms a firm ball. Wrap in cling film and refrigerate for 30 minutes.
2 Heat the oven to 200C/400F/Gas 6.
3 Roll out the pastry on a lightly floured surface and use to line a 25 cm/10 inch loose-bottomed flan tin. Refrigerate for 30 minutes.
4 Prick the base with a fork, line with greaseproof paper and weight down with baking beans. Bake in the oven for 10 minutes.
5 Remove paper and beans from pastry case, return to the oven and bake for a further 5 minutes.
6 Remove the pastry case from the tin and leave to cool on a wire rack for at least 2 hours.
7 Gently heat the jam with 1 tablespoon water and press through a sieve, then return to a small saucepan and bring to boil. Brush the inside of the pastry case with the jam. Reserve the remaining jam.
8 Sprinkle the gelatine over the remaining water in a heatproof bowl and leave to soak for 5 minutes until spongy. Stand bowl in a pan of gently simmering water and stir for 1-2 minutes until the gelatine has dissolved and the liquid is clear.

Cook's Notes

 TIME
About 1¼ hours to make, plus cooling and setting time.

COOK'S TIP
Do not refrigerate the flan: the strawberries are better at room temperature.

! WATCHPOINT
Do not allow the cream to become too thick, or it will be impossible to fold in the egg white.

VARIATION
Instead of spiking the top with pistachio nuts, try coating the sides with green coconut – use a plain flan tin then, before filling the flan, colour 40 g/1½ oz desiccated coconut with green food colouring. Brush the outside edge of the empty pastry case with extra hot jam, then roll in the coconut to coat. Sprinkle a little coconut on top if liked.

●760 calories/3175 kj per portion

9 Whisk the egg white until it stands in stiff peaks.
10 Put the cream with the sugar and vanilla in a bowl and whisk for a few seconds until frothy. ⬚ Pour the hot gelatine into the cream mixture in a thin stream, whisking until the cream thickens slightly, then quickly fold in the egg white.
11 Pour into the pastry case and spread evenly. Refrigerate for about 1 hour or until set.
12 Arrange the strawberries attractively on top of the set cream mixture. Bring the remaining jam back to the boil and brush over the strawberries to glaze.
13 Decorate the top of the flan with pistachios and cool before serving (see Cook's tip).

Parsley cheese bites

SERVES 4
75 g/3 oz full-fat soft cheese
100 g/4 oz Cheddar cheese, grated
50 g/2 oz Danish Blue cheese, at
  room temperature
freshly ground black pepper
4-5 tablespoons finely chopped
  fresh parsley
2-3 tablespoons plain flour

1 Work the cheeses together with a fork to form a smooth paste. Add pepper to taste.
2 Put the chopped parsley and flour on separate flat plates. Dip your hands in the flour, shaking off any excess, then shape the cheese mixture into 20 small balls, reflouring your hands as necessary. Roll each ball in chopped parsley.
3 Transfer to a serving plate and refrigerate for 30 minutes before serving. Serve chilled.

Cook's Notes

 TIME
Total preparation time is only 10-15 minutes but allow a further 30 minutes for chilling.

 VARIATIONS
Any mixture of cheese can be used and it is fun to experiment with different flavours, but the base must always be made from full-fat soft cheese to make the bites cling together. Try soft cheese flavoured with chives and, instead of Cheddar, use grated Wensleydale, Cheshire, Caerphilly or Lancashire cheese. A Blue Stilton or Italian Dolcelatte or Gorgonzola can be used in place of Danish Blue.

 SERVING IDEAS
Add these attractive little cheese bites to the cheeseboard at the end of the meal. Accompany them with cheese biscuits.

●250 calories/1025 kj per ball

Spicy barbecue lunch

Ideal for a leisurely lunch in the sun, this barbecue offers an exotic selection of three spicy dishes using marinated pork, chicken and lamb — guests pick and choose. Accompany the dishes with two unusual salads and finish with cooling water ice.

Curried pork

SERVES 12
3 pork fillets (tenderloins), total weight about 1.25 kg/2½ lb, trimmed and halved lengthways
vegetable oil, for greasing

MARINADE
8 tablespoons vegetable oil
2 tablespoons curry powder
2 tablespoons tomato purée
1 large onion, finely chopped
salt and freshly ground black pepper

1 First make the marinade: put the oil into a large bowl with the curry powder, tomato purée, onion and salt and pepper to taste. Mix well.
2 Cut each tenderloin half into bite-sized pieces.
3 Put the meat into the marinade and stir well to make sure each piece is well coated. Cover and marinate in a cool place for at least 3 hours.
4 Light the barbecue. Brush 12 kebab skewers with oil.
5 Thread the pork pieces on to the oiled skewers, reserving any marinade left in the bowl.
6 When the coals are hot, place the kebabs on the grid and cook for 12-15 minutes, turning and brushing with the reserved marinade, until the meat is cooked. Serve at once.

Chicken in yoghurt and ginger

SERVES 12
12 boned and skinned chicken breasts, each weighing 150 g/5 oz
vegetable oil, for brushing

MARINADE
300 g/10 oz natural yoghurt
2 tablespoons finely chopped fresh root ginger, or 2 teaspoons ground ginger
½ teaspoon ground cardamon
½ teaspoon cayenne pepper
2 tablespoons finely chopped fresh coriander or parsley
1 teaspoon salt
2 cloves garlic, crushed (optional)

1 Put all the marinade ingredients, including the garlic, if using, into a large bowl and stir well to mix.
2 Pat the chicken breasts dry with absorbent paper, then place in the marinade, making sure they are well coated. Cover and leave to marinate in a cool place for at least 3 hours.
3 Light the barbecue.
4 When the coals are hot, remove the chicken from marinade with a slotted spoon. Place the chicken on the grid and cook for 15-20 minutes, turning often and brushing with oil occasionally, until chicken is cooked. Serve at once.

Spiced lamb

SERVES 12
12 lean lamb chops, each weighing about 100 g/4 oz
vegetable oil, for brushing

DRY MARINADE
1 tablespoon finely chopped fresh root ginger, or 1 teaspoon ground ginger
2 cloves garlic, crushed (optional)
1 teaspoon ground cardamom
½ teaspoon ground cinnamon
1 teaspoon ground cumin
¼ teaspoon cayenne pepper
2 teaspoons ground turmeric
salt and freshly ground black pepper

1 First make the dry marinade: mix the ginger and garlic, if using, in a shallow dish with all the spices and plenty of salt and pepper.
2 Place the lamb chops in the dish and turn them in the spice mixture to make sure each chop is well coated. Cover the dish and leave to marinate in a cool place for at least 3 hours.
3 Light the barbecue.
4 When the coals are hot, place the chops on the grid and cook for 10-15 minutes, turning often and brushing with oil occasionally, until meat is cooked. Serve at once.

Cook's Notes

Curried pork
TIME
15 minutes to prepare, then at least 3 hours to marinate and 12-15 minutes cooking.

●235 calories/975 kj per portion

Chicken in yoghurt and ginger
TIME
10 minutes to prepare, then at least 3 hours to marinate, and 15-20 minutes cooking.

●190 calories/800 kj per portion

Spiced lamb
TIME
10 minutes to prepare, then at least 3 hours to marinate and 10-15 minutes cooking.

●175 calories/725 kj per portion

Coconut rice salad

SERVES 12
500 g/1 lb long-grain rice
salt
3 chicken stock cubes, crumbled
2 teaspoons cumin seeds
1 small coconut, broken open and
  flesh removed (see Preparation),
  or 225 g/8 oz packet shredded
  coconut
4 tablespoons corn or vegetable oil
2 tablespoons red wine vinegar
3 tablespoons finely chopped fresh
  parsley
¼ teaspoon mustard powder
freshly ground black pepper
3 bananas
175 g/6 oz salted peanuts

1 Fill a large saucepan with salted water and add the crumbled stock cubes. Bring to the boil, then add the rice and cumin seeds. Stir once to mix the ingredients together, then cover and simmer gently for 20-25 minutes until the rice is tender.
2 Pour the cooked rice into a colander and rinse well under cold running water. Leave to cool and drain well.
3 Meanwhile, grate the coconut flesh finely.
4 Put the oil in a large serving bowl with vinegar, parsley, mustard and pepper to taste. Mix well.
5 Just before serving: peel the bananas and slice them directly into the dressing. Mix lightly. Add the rice, grated coconut and peanuts ⚠ and fork lightly together. Serve the salad at once.

Cook's Notes

⏰ **TIME**
About 40 minutes to prepare, plus about 1 hour to prepare the coconut, most of which can be done while the rice is cooking.

❗ **WATCHPOINT**
Add the peanuts just before serving or they will go soggy if left to stand in the dressing for some time.

📓 **PREPARATION**
Before breaking open, make holes in 2-3 'eyes' of coconut with a screwdriver and drain off 'milk'.

● 385 calories/1600 kj per portion

Avocado and grapefruit salad

SERVES 12
3 small avocados
2 grapefruit
3 dessert apples
2 lettuces, separated into
  leaves

DRESSING
2 tablespoons clear honey
3 tablespoons cider vinegar
150 ml/¼ pint olive oil
salt and freshly ground black pepper

Cook's Notes

TIME
This salad takes 15 minutes to make.

WATCHPOINT
Always assemble this salad just before you wish to serve it, although you can make the dressing in advance and store in a covered container. The reason is that avocados tend to discolour slightly once they have been sliced even when incorporated in the dressing.
Also the dressing itself will make the lettuce limp if it is poured over too soon.

VARIATIONS
Use 4 large oranges in place of grapefruit. If you cannot buy cider vinegar, use white wine vinegar.

SERVING IDEAS
This refreshing and colourful salad, makes an excellent accompaniment to any barbecued meat.

●450 calories/1900 kj per portion

1 To make the dressing: mix together the honey, vinegar and olive oil in a bowl. Whisk with a fork until the dressing is thick and all the ingredients are thoroughly combined. Season to taste.
2 Peel the grapefruit. Hold over a bowl to catch the juice and, using a small, sharp knife, trim away any white pith. Divide the grapefruit into segments and remove the pips. Stir the segments into the dressing.
3 Halve the avocados lengthways, then remove the stones and peel. Slice the flesh and add immediately to the dressing. Toss thoroughly.
4 Quarter and core the apples. Slice them thinly and toss them in the dressing. Taste and adjust seasoning. Arrange the lettuce leaves in a salad bowl, pile the salad in the centre and serve at once.

Orange and lemon water-ice

SERVES 12
12 oranges (see Buying guide)
8-9 lemons
225 ml/8 fl oz water
450 g/1 lb sugar

1 Set the refrigerator or freezer at its coldest setting.
2 Wash the oranges and 3 of the lemons. With a potato peeler, peel the rinds from the 3 lemons thinly, then put them into a saucepan with the water and sugar. Stir over a low heat until the sugar has dissolved, then bring to the boil. Boil for 2 minutes, without stirring, then remove from the heat, cover and leave the syrup to stand for 1 hour.
3 Squeeze all the lemons and measure 450 ml/16 fl oz juice, making up the quantity with water if necessary. Cut the top third off each orange and carefully squeeze out the juice from the bottom two-thirds. ! Strain both lemon and orange juices together—you should have about 1.3 L/2¼ pints.
4 Remove all the remaining flesh from the orange cases (see Preparation). Put the orange cases and 'lids' on a tray (see Cook's tip) and put into the freezer.
5 Choose a very large bowl that will fit into the freezer compartment of a refrigerator or fast-freeze compartment of a freezer.
6 Pour the orange and lemon juice into the bowl then strain in the sugar syrup and stir well.
7 Freeze the juice for about 4 hours, until it has frozen to a width of 2.5 cm/1 inch around the edge, then remove from the freezer and stir well with a large metal spoon until evenly blended. Return to the freezer and freeze for a further 3 hours or until the water-ice is frozen to a firm mushy consistency, not completely hard. Stir with a metal spoon once every hour during this freezing process.
8 Fill the orange cases with the water-ice, mounding it up well on top. Replace the 'lids', pressing them in at an angle. Return the oranges to the freezer for 1-2 hours or until the water-ice is frozen.
9 When ready to serve, remove the oranges from the freezer and place on small decorative plates or saucers. Serve at once.

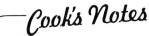

Cook's Notes

TIME
About 2 hours to make and 8-9 hours to freeze.

! WATCHPOINT
Be careful not to split the skins of the oranges when squeezing out the juice.

BUYING GUIDE
Choose oranges with good unmarked skins and try to find 12 more or less the same size.

COOK'S TIP
If the orange cases do not stand level, take a very thin slice off the bases.

PREPARATION
To remove all flesh from inside the oranges:

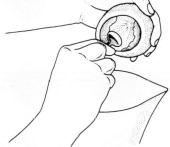

Use a teaspoon to scrape out all the flesh from the orange shells.

●190 calories/800 kj per portion

Beach-style barbecue

A whole fish cooked over a barbecue instantly conjures up the atmosphere of the beach and all the fun and frivolity that goes with it. Small spicy pies, eaten with the fingers, make an informal starter, while fruit kebabs complete the meal with a splash of colour.

Spicy vegetable pies

MAKES 12
350 g/12 oz shortcrust pastry
4 tablespoons olive oil
1 onion, finely chopped
3 cloves garlic, crushed (optional)
175 g/6 oz courgettes, diced
1 red pepper, deseeded and diced
75 g/3 oz tomato purée
½ teaspoon ground cumin
4 tablespoons chopped coriander
few drops of Tabasco
1 egg, beaten, to glaze

1 Make the filling: heat the oil in a large frying-pan, add the onion and garlic, if using, and fry gently for 5 minutes until the onion is soft and lightly coloured.
2 Add the diced courgettes and the red pepper and continue to cook for a further 2 minutes, stirring with a wooden spoon.
3 Stir in the tomato purée, cumin, coriander, Tabasco, and salt and pepper to taste. Continue to cook for a further 4 minutes, stirring constantly, then remove from the heat and cool for 10 minutes.
4 Heat the oven to 180C/350F/Gas 4.
5 Roll out the pastry very thinly on a lightly floured surface and cut out 12 rounds with a 9 cm/3½ inch plain cutter and 12 rounds with a 7.5 cm/3 inch cutter. Use larger rounds to line twelve deep 7.5 cm/3 inch bun tins. Reserve the remaining rounds for the pie lids.
6 Divide the filling between the pastry cases. Brush the edges of the remaining pastry rounds with water, and place on top of filled pastry cases. Press the edges of the lids to seal, then prick the tops.
7 Brush the top of each pie with beaten egg to glaze and bake in the oven for 30 minutes until the pastry tops are golden. Serve hot or cold.

Sea bass in a parcel

SERVES 6

1 fresh sea bass, weighing
   1.5-2 kg/3½-4½ lb (see Buying
   guide and Variations)
1 small bunch fresh dill or fennel
   leaves, finely chopped
½ fennel bulb, weighing about
   150 g/5 oz, finely chopped
salt and freshly ground black pepper
1 onion, finely chopped
2 carrots, finely chopped
2 lemons, skinned and sliced
75 ml/3 fl oz dry vermouth
2 tablespoons olive oil
dill sprigs, to garnish (optional)

1 Light the barbecue. Mix half the chopped dill with the chopped fennel bulb and season to taste with salt and pepper. Stuff the cavity of the fish with this mixture.
2 Fold a large piece of foil in half to make a rectangle twice as long and three times as wide as the fish.
3 Sprinkle the onion, carrots and remaining dill down the centre of the foil to make a bed for the fish.
4 Place the fish on top of the bed of vegetables, then arrange the lemon slices along the fish.
5 Bring up the long edges of the foil to meet over the fish, but do not seal. Pinch the short edges together, then fold to seal, to form a boat shape. Pour the vermouth and oil over the fish, then seal the long edges of the foil together, leaving plenty of room inside for the steam to circulate.
6 When the coals are hot, carefully place the foil-wrapped fish on the barbecue grid and cook for about 10 minutes per 500 g/1 lb or until the flesh flakes easily when tested with a knife.
7 Transfer fish to a long dish and carefully open up the foil. Garnish with dill. To serve: cut along the length of one side to remove fillets. Repeat on other side.

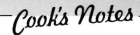

Cook's Notes

Spicy vegetable pies

TIME
30 minutes preparation;
30 minutes cooking.

DID YOU KNOW
These tasty vegetable pies are a simplified version of a Caribbean recipe.

● 180 calories/750 kj per pie

Sea bass in a parcel

TIME
20 minutes preparation;
about 1 hour cooking.

BUYING GUIDE
Sea bass is in season from later summer until April. Order the fish in advance from a good fishmonger, and ask him to clean the fish without slitting it completely along the belly; this way it retains a good shape during cooking.

VARIATIONS
If sea bass is difficult to obtain, try serving each person with their own individually-wrapped small fish. In this case, each fish should weigh about 350 g/12 oz. Choose from grey mullet, sea trout or mackerel and cook over a barbecue for a slightly shorter length of time.

SERVING IDEAS
Corn on the cob makes a perfect accompaniment to the fish and can be cooked over the barbecue with great success — soak unhusked corn on the cob in salted cold water for 1 hour, then drain and roast on the grid for 10-15 minutes. Alternatively, cook the husked corn spread with a flavoured butter and wrapped in foil (see page 42).
Jacket-baked potatoes, wrapped in foil and cooked in the barbecue coals are another good accompaniment.
For a green vegetable, serve a simple green salad.

● 270 calories/1125 kj per portion

Spiced corn on the cob

SERVES 6
6 corn on the cob

SPICED BUTTER
175 g/6 oz salted butter, softened
¼ teaspoon freshly grated nutmeg
¼ teaspoon sweet paprika
1 teaspoon ground cinnamon
2 teaspoons lemon juice

1 Light the barbecue.
2 Make the spiced butter: beat the butter in a bowl with the spices and lemon juice.
3 Remove the husks and silky threads from the corn. Place each cob on a double square of foil and spread with the butter mixture. Wrap up foil and fold to seal.
4 When the coals are hot, place the corn in coals for 15-20 minutes. Remove from foil and serve at once, with the buttery juice poured over.

 TIME
10 minutes to prepare the corn and spiced butter, 5 minutes to assemble and 15-20 minutes cooking.

 BUYING GUIDE
Choose young cobs with pale, golden-yellow kernels and green, fresh leaves. Cook as soon as possible after buying as the kernels quickly become wrinkled and taste dry and leathery.

 DID YOU KNOW
America was, of course, Christopher Columbus' big discovery—sweetcorn was one his lesser-known ones! He brought it back to Europe from South America and it became widely used to make cornmeal for bread and cake making. Sweetcorn is sometimes known as maize or Indian corn.

 COOK'S TIP
If fresh corn is not available, use frozen corn on the cob — put in boiling water, bring back to the boil, then drain at once. Place on the squares of foil and spread with the butter mixture.

 SERVING IDEAS
If wished, make extra spiced butter to serve with the cooked corn.
The cobs may be eaten by holding either end with your fingers. To make eating easier, however, insert specially-designed corn on the cob holders into either end of each cob: these allow you to hold the cob without burning your fingers. Remember to provide plenty of paper napkins for wiping buttery fingers.

●265 calories/1115 kj per cob

Carnival fruit kebabs

SERVES 6
1 small pineapple
3 oranges
3 dessert apples
3 firm bananas
6 apricots, halved and stoned
1 bunch large black grapes

BUTTER SAUCE
100 g/4 oz butter
1 tablespoon light soft brown sugar
1 teaspoon ground cardamom
1 tablespoon lemon juice

1 Twist leaves off the pineapple, then slice off the skin, taking care to cut deeply enough to remove all the black 'whiskers'. Slice the pineapple, then cut into even-sized chunks, removing any tough, woody core.

2 Peel the oranges with a sharp knife and remove all the pith. Divide each orange into 6 segments. Quarter and core the apples, then cut into chunks. Peel the bananas and cut into 2.5 cm/1 inch lengths (see Cook's tip).

3 Put the pieces of pineapple, orange, apple, banana and apricot on to 12 skewers, threading a grape between each piece.

4 Make the butter sauce: over the dying barbecue coals, melt the butter in a small saucepan. Add the brown sugar, cardamom and lemon juice and stir until the ingredients are well blended.

6 Place the skewers of fruit on the grid over the dying barbecue coals, brush liberally with the butter sauce and cook for 5 minutes turning frequently and brushing with more butter sauce. Serve at once.

SUMMER
ENTERTAINING

Get carried away with the carefree mood of summer and throw parties galore for family and friends — the image of relaxing over a delightfully lazy meal during a long hot summer's day is quite irresistible!

Our exciting selection of menus gives you lots of ideas for unusual summer parties. Platters of cold meat and various salads are all very

delicious, but you should allow scope for hot meals as well. Our menus offer both hot and cold food — we take full advantage of the plentiful fresh summer produce around to create luscious spreads for all to enjoy. The recipes featured make light work of cooking, so that you do not have to spend hours slaving over a hot stove, and the menu planning is such that many dishes can be made in advance. Where appropriate, there are countdown timetables to help you get you through your party without a hitch. With our party menus there is no need to greet your guests in a hot and flustered state!

Outdoor parties

Eating outdoors is one of the pleasures of summer. It is the perfect way to make the most of the warm weather. However, as with all parties, much of the success depends upon sensible planning. Our outdoor menus have been specially chosen to avoid all the pitfalls of serving food outside.

Food for eating outdoors must be easy to serve. Items should be carved into slices in advance, if possible, and dishes which crumble or disintegrate easily should be avoided. Another important point is that the food must be uncomplicated to eat — fork food is ideal. If knives and forks are called for, make sure that there are sufficient small tables for guests to rest their plates against.

Outdoor parties are usually relaxed easy-going affairs, calling for suitably informal dishes. But this does not mean that more lavish meals are out of the question — our buffet dinner party, offering a sumptuous fish salad and a glamorous strawberry charlotte, creates an elegant occasion without much effort. The patio party is another impressive menu — refreshing Parma ham and melon, followed by delicate veal rolls and a glorious ice cream bombe, make up this delicious spread.

On the informal side, there is a delicious lunch-time spread, based around savoury flans. Ideal fare for outdoor entertaining, flans can be served hot or cold and can be neatly sliced up for serving. Sunday brunch is a marvellous idea for

getting the maximum enjoyment out of the weekend, while a family picnic is a classic summertime occasion, which allows for spontaneous additions of your own, if you wish.

Indoor parties

If the weather lets you down, or you simply do not have the means to entertain outdoors, you can bring the spirit of summer into your home with our inspired party menus.

For a relaxing, help-yourself evening, there is a fondue party. Eaten at a slow pace, the food is suitably light-weight for hot weather and, of course, everyone does their own cooking, releasing you from the confines of the kitchen.

Taking a tip from Far Eastern countries, hot spicy food is often a great idea for stimulating appetites during sizzling weather — our exotic curry lunch is sure to go down well with family and friends alike.

Dinner parties with Caribbean and Californian themes instantly conjure up a laid-back, sunny mood, while a sophisticated French dinner party will take you back to those happy holiday moments.

Salads

Take a fresh look at salads and discover the variety and colour they can bring to summer meals. In the section on salads, we suggest not only delicious side salads, but also a wealth of salad appetizers and substantial main courses, plus two refreshing fruit salad ideas.

Drinks parties

Ice-cold exotic drinks are a real treat for hot summer days or warm, sultry evenings. Serve icy alcoholic drinks with a choice of tasty nibbles and you instantly have a drinks party on your hands. The blissful thing about drinks parties is that the preparation is minimal and the organisation is easy — tremendous for summer entertaining. To make life even simpler for you, we have suggested a selection of drinks party menus, offering loads of icy, alcoholic thirst-quenchers and a great variety of nibbles and light snacks to serve with the drinks.

The parties range from a Spanish sangria evening to an impressive Champagne party — and you can learn how to mix a mean cocktail!

OUTDOOR PARTIES
Pitta party

Pitta, the flat unleavened bread from the Middle East, provides a marvellous base for an informal outdoor party. Served hot and cut into fingers, it is perfect for dipping, or it can be cut in half or slit lengthways to make a handy container for our imaginative fillings. Sweetmeats and fruit salad make the ideal follow-up.

COUNTDOWN
The day before
● Make the mackerel dip, cover and refrigerate.
● Prepare the sweetmeats and store in an airtight tin.
3 hours before the meal
● Make the caramel sauce and prepare cream for fruit salads.
● Place lamb cubes in marinade.

● Prepare the vegetables for the salads and make the dressings.
30 minutes before
● Take mackerel dip out of the refrigerator.
● Begin to make the omelette strips.
20 minutes before
● Begin to grill the kebabs.
15 minutes before
● Pour dressings over the 2 salads and toss well.
5-10 minutes before
● Place 20 pitta breads wrapped in foil in a 180C/350F/Gas 4 oven.
Just before the dessert
● Assemble the fruit salads.

Creamy smoked mackerel dip

SERVES 8
500 g/1 lb smoked mackerel fillets, skinned
juice of 2 lemons
150 ml/¼ pint soured cream
freshly ground black pepper
chopped parsley, to garnish

1 Flake the mackerel flesh into a bowl, removing as many bones as possible. Add the lemon juice, soured cream and pepper to taste.
2 Beat well with a wooden spoon until the mixture is smooth and creamy.
3 Put the mixture in a serving dish and garnish with chopped parsley. Serve with hot 'fingers' of pitta bread for dipping.

Cook's Notes

TIME
Preparation time is about 15 minutes.

COOK'S TIP
The dip can be made up to 24 hours ahead of time and stored in the refrigerator, covered with cling film. Bring to room temperature for 30 minutes before serving.

VARIATION
Use smoked trout instead of mackerel.

●185 calories/775 kj per portion

Party kebabs

SERVES 8
1 kg/2 lb lean lamb (from the leg or shoulder), trimmed of fat and cut into 2.5 cm/1 inch cubes
1 green pepper, deseeded and cut into 2.5 cm/1 inch squares
16-24 mushrooms
lemon wedges, to garnish
vegetable oil, for greasing

MARINADE
150 ml/¼ pint olive oil
juice of 2 lemons
1 bay leaf, crushed
1 teaspoon dried oregano
salt and freshly ground black pepper

1 To make the marinade: mix together in a large bowl the oil, lemon juice and herbs. Season with salt and pepper to taste.
2 Put the lamb cubes into the marinade and turn to coat well. Cover with cling film and leave for 2-3 hours in a cool place.
3 Heat the grill to moderate.
4 Remove meat from the marinade with a slotted spoon and drain on absorbent paper. Thread the meat, green pepper and mushrooms evenly between 8 oiled skewers.
5 Grill for about 20 minutes, turning to cook all sides.
6 Using a fork, push the meat and vegetables off the skewers and on to a warmed serving platter. Garnish with lemon wedges. Use to fill pitta bread 'pockets' or serve separately.

Cheese and tomato omelette strips

SERVES 8
3 eggs
1 tablespoon water
50 g/2 oz Cheddar cheese, grated
2 tomatoes, skinned, deseeded and roughly chopped
pinch of dried mixed herbs
salt and freshly ground black pepper
15 g/½ oz butter

1 Break the eggs into a bowl, add the water and beat lightly with a fork. Add the cheese, tomatoes, herbs and salt and pepper to taste. Beat the mixture lightly again to mix well.
2 Heat the grill to moderate.
3 Melt the butter in a frying-pan over moderate heat. Swirl it over the base and sides of the pan. When the butter is sizzling, lower the heat and pour the egg mixture into the pan. Cook for 3 minutes, drawing the mixture from sides to middle so that the uncooked egg runs over the hot pan.
4 Place the pan under the hot grill and cook the top of the omelette for a further 2 minutes, or until set and lightly browned. Do not overcook the omelette otherwise it will be much too dry.
5 Remove from the grill and allow to cool for 5 minutes. Cut into long strips about 1 cm/½ inch wide and set aside on a warmed serving platter, ready for guests to pack into the pitta bread.

Cook's Notes

Party kebabs

TIME
Preparation and cooking take about 30 minutes, but remember to allow 2-3 hours for marinating the meat.

VARIATION
Boned leg of pork also makes delicious kebabs, cook for 5 minutes longer.
If wished, cook the kebabs on a barbecue.

●290 calories/1200 kj per portion

Omelette strips

TIME
Preparation and cooking take about 20 minutes in total.

VARIATIONS
A wide variety of other flavourings can be used such as chopped ham, cooked diced potato, sliced fried mushrooms, chopped fried bacon or sweetcorn.

●70 calories/300 kj per portion

Cucumber and pepper salad

SERVES 8
2 cucumbers, peeled and cut into
   1 cm/½ inch cubes
2 red peppers, deseeded and cut
   into 1 cm/½ inch squares
3 tablespoons snipped chives
20 black olives, halved and stoned,
   to garnish

DRESSING
6 tablespoons olive oil
2 tablespoons white wine vinegar
2 tablespoons natural yoghurt
salt and freshly ground black pepper

1 Mix together the cucumbers, red peppers and chives in a shallow bowl.
2 To make the dressing: put the olive oil, vinegar and yoghurt in a screw-top jar. Season to taste.
3 When ready to serve, shake the dressing to mix it well, pour over the salad and toss to coat thoroughly. Garnish the top of the salad with the olive halves.

Crunchy cabbage salad

SERVES 8
½ large white cabbage, finely
   shredded
1 onion, thinly sliced
1 punnet mustard and cress

DRESSING
4 tablespoons olive oil
2 tablespoons lemon juice
salt and freshly ground black pepper

1 Mix the cabbage and onion together in a salad bowl.
2 Trim the cress, and add to the cabbage and onion mixture in the salad bowl.
3 To make the dressing: put the olive oil and lemon juice into a screw-top jar, with salt and pepper to taste.
4 When ready to serve, shake the dressing to mix it well, then pour over the cabbage salad and toss to coat thoroughly.

Fruit salad specials

SERVES 8
600 ml/1 pint double cream
5 teaspoons Strega liqueur (see Did you know and Variations)
225 g/8 oz strawberries, hulled
3 bananas
3 dessert apples
100 g/4 oz green grapes, halved and deseeded

CARAMEL SAUCE
200 g/7 oz caster sugar
8 tablespoons water

1 Make the caramel sauce: put the caster sugar in a small, heavy-based saucepan together with 2 table-spoons water. Heat very gently, until the sugar has dissolved. Bring to the boil and boil rapidly without stirring, until the syrup turns a rich caramel colour.
2 Remove from the heat and add the remaining water, 1 tablespoon at a time, taking care as it will splutter when the water is added to the very hot caramel. Stir well together, returning to the heat if necessary, until well blended. Set aside to cool for about 2½ hours.
3 Whip the cream until standing in soft peaks, then fold in the liqueur (see Cook's tip). Divide between 8 individual shallow glass dishes, about 12.5 cm/5 inches in diameter, and smooth over top with a knife. Cover and refrigerate for at least 1-2 hours.
4 Just before serving, slice the strawberries, slice the bananas, then core and slice the apples. Arrange, with the grapes, in neat rows on top of the chilled cream and carefully coat with the caramel sauce. Serve the fruit salad at once.

Cook's Notes

TIME
45 minutes preparation, plus cooling the syrup and chilling the cream, then 10 minutes finishing the salad.

DID YOU KNOW
Strega is a sweet, citrus liqueur from Italy.

 VARIATIONS
Use different varieties of fruit or liqueur to taste – apricot- or cherry-flavoured liqueurs are both suitable.

 COOK'S TIP
Sugar is not added to the cream – the caramel sauce sweetens the dish.

WATCHPOINT
It is important not to stir the syrup while it is boiling as this may crystallize the caster sugar. Watch the caramel carefully – if it is too dark, it will taste strong and rather bitter.

●525 calories/2200 kj per portion

Middle Eastern sweetmeats

MAKES ABOUT 40 PASTRIES
450 g/1 lb plain flour
225 g/8 oz unsalted butter, diced
2 tablespoons rosewater or orange-
  flower water
3 tablespoons milk
175 g/6 oz icing sugar, sifted

1 Make the fillings (see below) and leave them to cool.
2 Heat the oven to 170C/325F/Gas 3. Sift the flour into a large bowl. Add the butter and work into the flour with your fingertips until crumbly. Add the rosewater and milk to make a soft, easily handled dough.
3 Take a piece of dough the size of a walnut. Roll it into a ball between your hands. Hollow the ball out with your thumb and pinch up the sides. Shape the remainder of the dough in the same way and fill half the balls with date filling and the other half with nut filling. Press the dough back over the filling, pinching it together to seal. Decorate the tops with the prongs of a fork (see Cook's tip).
4 Arrange the pastries on a large baking sheet and bake in oven for 20-25 minutes. Do not brown. ⚠ Leave to cool on baking sheet.
5 When the pastries are quite cold, roll them in sifted icing sugar and serve in small paper cases.

DATE FILLING
250 g/9 oz stoned dates (see Buying guide)
75 ml/3 fl oz water

1 Put the dates in a saucepan with the water. Cook gently over very low heat, stirring frequently, until the dates are soft and pulpy.
2 Leave to cool before using to fill half the pastries.

NUT FILLING
100 g/4 oz walnuts, chopped
75 100 g/3 4 oz sugar
1 teaspoon ground cinnamon

1 Mix the nuts with sugar to taste and stir in the cinnamon.
2 Mix very thoroughly before using to fill the remaining pastries.

Cook's Notes

TIME
Preparation about 45 minutes, baking 20-25 minutes, making the fillings 20 minutes and finishing the pastries 5-10 minutes.

COOK'S TIP
Making a ridged pattern on the pastries helps the icing sugar to stick.

BUYING GUIDE
Packages of dried pressed dates, readily available from supermarkets, are best for this recipe.

WATCHPOINT
On no account allow the pastries to brown, or they will be hard. When taken from the oven they will look soft and uncooked, but in fact will firm up when they have completely cooled.

SERVING IDEAS
Serve these pastries with small squares of Turkish delight for an authentic Middle Eastern effect.

● 130 calories/550 kj (date pastry)
● 145 calories/600 kj (walnut pastry)

Enjoy warm summer evenings to the full and treat a group of your friends to a rather special meal on the patio. This menu looks elegant, but is very practical for serving outdoors: melon and Parma ham chunks on skewers can be eaten barbecue-style, while veal rolls are neat to serve. A glorious ice cream bombe, whipped out of the freezer at the last moment, will create a cool surprise as a dessert.

Melon with Parma ham starter

SERVES 8
2 sweet melons (see Buying guide)
8 thin slices Parma ham (see Buying guide)
freshly ground black pepper

1 Cut the melons into quarters and scoop out the seeds. Carefully slice flesh away from skin, then cut each quarter into 6 even-sized chunks.
2 Trim fatty edge of parma ham, then cut each slice into 6 pieces.
3 Wrap a piece of Parma ham round each melon chunk. Thread 6 chunks on to each of 8 skewers.
4 Refrigerate for up to 2 hours. Before serving, sprinkle with pepper.

Party veal rolls

SERVES 8
8 thin veal escalopes
100 g/4 oz butter
4 streaky bacon rashers, rinds removed, coarsely chopped
1 courgette, peeled and finely chopped
100 g/4 oz mushrooms, finely chopped
175 g/6 oz Ricotta cheese (see Buying guide)
75 g/3 oz fresh brown breadcrumbs
juice of ½ lemon
½ teaspoon dried oregano
salt and freshly ground black pepper
3 tablespoons dry vermouth
tomato skin roses and parsley sprigs, to garnish (see Preparation)

Cook's Notes

Melon with Parma ham starter

TIME
This refreshing starter takes only 15 minutes to make.

BUYING GUIDE
Buy ogen or cantaloupe melons and make sure that they are really ripe – the flesh should give slightly under the pressure of your thumb, and the perfume should be quite strong.
Parma ham is available from Italian delicatessens – check that the ham is not cut from an end piece, otherwise the slices will be too small and probably rather dry.

SERVING IDEAS
Add a touch of informality to the meal and suggest that guests slide the chunks off the skewers with their fingers.

●40 calories/175 kj per portion

Party veal rolls

TIME
45 minutes preparation, 15 minutes cooking.

BUYING GUIDE
Ricotta is a soft fresh Italian cheese, and is sold in delicatessens. If difficult to obtain, cottage cheese is the nearest substitute; sieve before adding to the blender.

COOK'S TIP
Spread the paste down the centre of the veal, so that it does not ooze out of the sides when you are rolling up the escalopes.

PREPARATION
To make a tomato skin rose garnish:

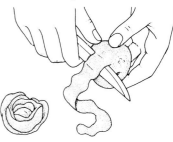

Put a tomato into a pan of boiling water for 1 minute, drain and thinly pare off the skin, cutting in a spiral motion. Wind up the skin to form a rose shape.

SERVING IDEAS
Serve the veal rolls on a bed of pasta shells and accompany the dish with a brightly-coloured mixed salad.

●365 calories/1525 kj per portion

1 Melt 25 g/1 oz butter in a frying-pan, add the bacon and fry gently for 5 minutes. Remove from the pan with a slotted spoon and set aside.
2 Add chopped courgette and mushrooms to remaining fat and cook over low heat until tender.
3 Transfer the courgette and mushrooms to the goblet of a blender, add the bacon, cheese, breadcrumbs, lemon juice and oregano and blend to a smooth paste. Season to taste with salt and pepper.
4 Place the veal escalopes between 2 sheets of greaseproof paper and beat with a wooden rolling pin or mallet until flattened out to about twice their original size.
5 Spread each escalope with the paste (see Cook's tip), then roll up and secure firmly with wooden cocktail sticks or, alternatively, tie the rolls at both ends with string.
6 Melt the remaining butter in a heavy-based frying-pan large enough to hold the rolls in a single layer. When the butter is foaming, add the rolls and cook gently for about 6 minutes until they are browned on all sides.
7 Spoon over the vermouth, bring the liquid to the boil, then lower the heat, cover and cook very gently for about 15 minutes or until the veal is completely tender.
8 Transfer the veal rolls to a warmed serving dish with a slotted spoon (see Serving ideas). Remove the cocktail sticks or string, then pour the pan juices over the rolls. Garnish with tomato skin roses and parsley sprigs and serve at once.

Mixed salad with hot dressing

SERVES 8

1 large lettuce (see Buying guide)
1 bunch radishes, trimmed
350 g/12 oz peas, unshelled weight
  (see Buying guide)

DRESSING
100 g/4 oz butter
1 tablespoon lemon juice
salt and freshly ground black pepper

1 Roughly tear up the lettuce and put into a salad bowl.
2 Slice the radishes and add them to the lettuce together with the shelled peas.
3 Make the dressing: melt butter in a small saucepan over very low heat. Stir in the lemon juice and season to taste.
4 Pour the dressing on to the salad while it is still warm. Toss the salad with dressing and serve at once. [!]

Cook's Notes

 TIME
This summery salad only takes about 10 minutes to make.

 SERVING IDEAS
An unusual combination of a hot dressing with cold vegetables, this makes an excellent side salad. It provides a crisp contrast to the veal rolls.
  If liked, garnish with sprinkling of crumbled, crisply-fried bacon or bread croûtons fried in butter, oil and garlic.

VARIATION
Try adding 100 g/4 oz thinly sliced button mushrooms and a few sliced spring onions with the radishes and peas and serve as a salad snack, with wholemeal rolls.

 BUYING GUIDE
Use a crisp lettuce such as a cos, iceberg or Webb's Wonder.
  This quantity of unshelled peas will produce about 175 g/6 oz peas after shelling. If fresh peas are unavailable, use 175 g/6 oz defrosted frozen peas.

[!] WATCHPOINT
Serve the salad immediately, otherwise the hot dressing will make the lettuce go limp very quickly.

● 220 calories/925 kj per portion

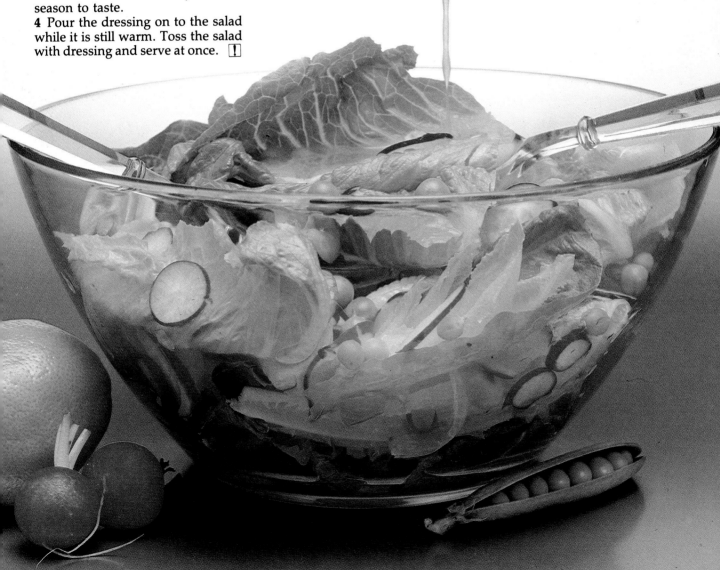

Ginger and coffee bombe

SERVES 8
425 ml/¾ pint coffee ice cream
150 ml/¼ pint whipped cream
crystallized ginger and angelica

GINGER ICE CREAM
4 eggs, separated
100 g/4 oz icing sugar
2 tablespoons brandy
300 ml/½ pint double cream
75 g/3 oz drained stem ginger,
    chopped

1 To make the ginger ice cream: in a clean, dry bowl, whisk the egg whites until they stand in stiff peaks, then gradually whisk in the icing sugar, 1 tablespoon at a time.
2 Stir the brandy into the cream, then whisk until in soft peaks.
3 Whisk the egg yolks in a large bowl until frothy, then fold in the egg white mixture. Gently stir in the whipped brandy-flavoured cream.
4 Pour the ice cream mixture into a freezerproof container and sprinkle the chopped ginger over the top. ⚠ Cover and freeze overnight.
5 Put a 1 L/2 pint bombe mould (see Buying guide) into the freezer and freeze overnight.
6 The next day, beat the coffee ice cream until just soft, ⚠ then put 2 tablespoons in chilled mould. Hold mould with a tea-towel; spread and press the ice cream over the base. Working from the base to the rim, smooth the rest of the ice cream into the mould to form a lining about 2.5 cm/1 inch thick.
7 Cover the mould and return to the freezer for at least 1 hour.
8 Remove the ginger ice cream from the freezer and allow to soften at room temperature for about 10 minutes. Spoon into the centre of the lined mould, pressing down firmly. Smooth the surface with the back of a spoon, cover and return to the freezer for 2-3 hours.

9 To serve: dip the mould in hot water (see Cook's tip), then invert a plate on top. Hold the mould and plate firmly together and invert. Pipe cream around base and decorate with ginger and angelica. Return to the freezer for up to 1 hour.

Cook's Notes

TIME
30 minutes to make the ginger ice cream, then overnight freezing. 30 minutes to finish the bombe, plus 3-4 hours freezing.

BUYING GUIDE
Bombe moulds can be bought at good kitchen equipment shops. As an alternative, you can use a pudding basin.

WATCHPOINTS
Do not fold in ginger, as it will very gradually sink into the ice cream during freezing.
    The ice cream should be just soft enough to work – not too runny.

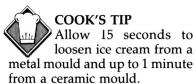

COOK'S TIP
Allow 15 seconds to loosen ice cream from a metal mould and up to 1 minute from a ceramic mould.

●400 calories/1675 kj per portion

Buffet lunch

Create a holiday atmosphere with this easy buffet lunch for ten. Ever popular salads and quiches are the theme — uncomplicated food, that is ideal for serving outdoors. Together, the four quiches will serve ten generously: cut each into slender wedges to give everyone a taste. The fruit salads will provide enough for everybody to have a half serving of each — perfect with a slice of ice box pudding.

COUNTDOWN
The day before
● Make the Rice salad and Courgette and carrot vinaigrette. Cover with cling film and leave in a cool place.
● Make the quiches. When cold, transfer them to serving plates, cover with cling film and leave in a cool place.
● Make the Pears and prunes in white wine, cover and refrigerate. Prepare the lemon curls for decoration, cover with cling film and refrigerate.
● Make the Mixed fruit delight, omitting the bananas. Cover and refrigerate.
● Make the Lime ice box pudding and freeze.
● Assemble cutlery, napkins and glasses. Check that you have enough chairs and small tables suitable for use outdoors.

In the morning
● Remove fruit desserts from the refrigerator and allow to come to room temperature. Sprinkle the Pears and prunes in white wine with lemon curls.
● Garnish the Rice salad.
● Cut the quiches into wedges, garnish and re-cover.
● Prepare a fresh green salad but do not dress it.

Just before the party
● Dress and toss the green salad.
● Whip the cream.
● Add the bananas to the Mixed fruit delight.
● Unmould ice box pudding.

Rice salad

SERVES 10
500 g/1 lb long-grain rice
1 cucumber, cut into 1 cm/½ inch dice
salt
4 tomatoes, deseeded and diced
1 red or green pepper, deseeded and diced
50 g/2 oz flaked almonds
75 g/2 oz seedless raisins

DRESSING
4 tablespoons vegetable oil
4 teaspoons lemon juice
¾ teaspoon ground ginger
freshly ground black pepper

TO GARNISH
about 20 black olives, halved and stoned (optional)
¼-½ cucumber, halved lengthways and thinly sliced (optional)

1 Put the diced cucumber into a colander set on a tray or large plate. Sprinkle with salt and leave to stand for 30 minutes, to allow the cucumber to drain.
2 Meanwhile, cook the rice in plenty of boiling salted water for 12-15 minutes until tender, then rinse well under hot running water to separate the grains.
3 Put the drained rice while it is still warm into a large bowl and add the tomatoes, red pepper, almonds and raisins. Pat the cucumber dry with absorbent paper and add to the salad, then fold gently to mix.
4 Put all the dressing ingredients into a screw-top jar with salt and pepper to taste. Shake to mix thoroughly. Pour over the warm rice salad and stir in gently. Leave the salad to cool, then cover and keep in a cool place until required.
5 To garnish: transfer to a large shallow serving dish. Arrange the halved olives around the edge and scatter the cucumber slices on top, if wished.

Courgette and carrot vinaigrette

SERVES 10

1 kg/2 lb small carrots, cut into
   matchstick strips
salt
1 kg/2 lb small courgettes, cut into
   matchstick strips

DRESSING
5 tablespoons vegetable oil or olive
   oil
2 tablespoons white wine vinegar
2-3 tablespoons finely chopped
   parsley
freshly ground black pepper
½ teaspoon ground coriander
   (optional)

1 Put the carrots into a pan of boiling salted water, return to boiling point and simmer for 8 minutes, or until just tender. Drain in a colander, rinse under cold running water and drain again thoroughly.

2 Meanwhile, plunge the courgettes into a pan of boiling salted water. Return to boiling point and simmer for about 3 minutes, or until just tender.

3 Drain the courgettes well in a colander, rinse under cold running water and drain thoroughly. Transfer both the courgettes and the carrots to a large flat dish.

4 Put all the dressing ingredients into a screw-top jar with salt and pepper to taste and the coriander, if using. Shake thoroughly to mix.

5 Pour the dressing over the vegetables while they are still warm (see Cook's tip), then turn with a large metal spoon until evenly coated with dressing. Leave to cool, then cover until required.

6 To serve: spoon the courgettes and carrots into 1 or 2 serving dishes, then pour over any dressing remaining in the dish.

Cook's Notes

TIME
Preparation and cooking time is 40-50 minutes.

COOK'S TIP
Warm vegetables will absorb more dressing.

●95 calories/400 kj per portion

Quiche quartet

BASIC QUICHE

MAKES 4

750 g/1½ lb shortcrust pastry,
   defrosted if frozen
4 quantities filling (see below)
8 eggs
600 ml/1 pint milk
lightly beaten egg white, to seal

1 Heat the oven to 200C/400F/Gas 6.
2 Roll out the pastry on a floured surface and use it to line four 20 cm/ 8 inch ceramic flan dishes ✳ or flan rings set on baking sheets (see Cook's tips). ! Prick each base with a fork. Place a large circle of grease-proof paper or foil in each pastry case and weight it down with baking beans.
3 Bake in the oven for 10 minutes. Remove the paper and beans, brush the insides of the pastry cases with beaten egg white, then return to the oven for a further 5 minutes.
4 Spoon the chosen fillings into the pastry cases, distributing them evenly. In a large bowl, beat together the eggs and the milk with a fork. Pour one-quarter of the egg and milk mixture evenly over each filling.
5 Return to the oven and bake for about 35 minutes until set and golden.

BACON, MUSHROOM AND PARSLEY FILLING

MAKES A 20 CM/8 INCH QUICHE

100 g/4 oz unsmoked streaky bacon,
   rinds removed, cut into strips
100 g/4 oz button mushrooms,
   thinly sliced
1-2 tablespoons chopped fresh
   parsley
salt and freshly ground black
   pepper
75 ml/3 fl oz milk
tomato wedges and parsley sprigs,
   to garnish

1 Heat a frying-pan without fat over low heat. Add the bacon and fry over moderate heat, stirring, for 2 minutes. Add the mushrooms and fry for a further 1-2 minutes until slightly softened.
2 Remove the pan from the heat and stir in the parsley. Season to taste with salt and pepper. Set aside to cool slightly, then spread the bacon and mushroom filling in the pre-pared pastry case.
3 Add the milk to one-quarter of the basic egg and milk mixture, then pour over the filling. Bake as in basic recipe.
4 Serve warm or cold, garnished with the tomato wedges and parsley sprigs.

CHICKEN AND WALNUT FILLING

MAKES A 20 CM/8 INCH QUICHE

250 g/9 oz cooked chicken, finely
   chopped (see Buying guide)
50 g/2 oz shelled walnuts, roughly
   chopped
100 g/4 oz Gruyere cheese, finely
   grated
large pinch of freshly grated
   nutmeg
salt and freshly ground black pepper
watercress sprigs, to garnish

1 Mix the chicken with the walnuts and half the cheese. Add nutmeg and season with salt and pepper.
2 Spread the mixture evenly in the prepared case and pour over one-quarter of the basic egg and milk mixture.
3 Sprinkle the remaining cheese on top of the filling, then bake as in basic recipe.
4 Serve warm or cold, cut into wedges and garnished with watercress sprigs.

Cook's Notes

Basic quiche

TIME
If you bake the quiches 2 at a time, the total cooking time will be about 2 hours. The exact preparation time will depend on your choice of filling and whether you use fresh or frozen pastry.

! **WATCHPOINT**
If using a flan ring, make sure that the pastry case has no cracks or holes or the filling will run out. Patch up any cracks with pastry scraps dampened on one side and pressed into place with your fingertips.

COOK'S TIPS
If you do not have 4 flan dishes to cook 4 quiches together, you can use 2 flan rings. Remove them while quiches are still hot, cool quiches on a wire rack and wash, dry and re-use rings immediately.

✳ **FREEZING**
Bake the quiches in foil flan dishes, then cool quickly. Cover, seal, label and freeze. Store for 3 months. To serve: uncover and defrost for 3 hours at room temperature.

● 1035 calories/4350 kj per quiche

Bacon, mushroom and parsley filling

TIME
Preparation 20 minutes, cooking 35 minutes.

● 375 calories/1575 kj per portion

Chicken and walnut filling

TIME
Preparation 25 minutes, cooking 35 minutes.

BUYING GUIDE
A 500 g/1 lb ready-roasted chicken half will supply enough meat.

● 515 calories/2150 kj per portion

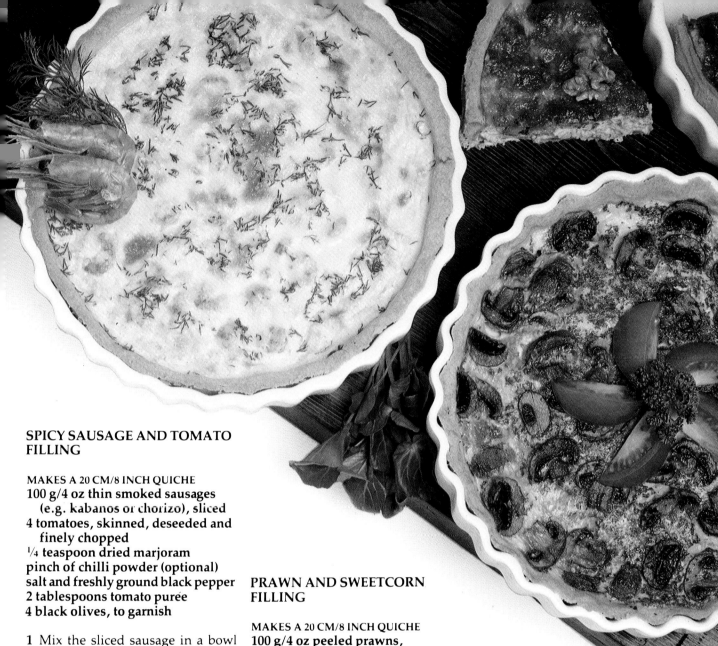

SPICY SAUSAGE AND TOMATO FILLING

MAKES A 20 CM/8 INCH QUICHE
100 g/4 oz thin smoked sausages (e.g. kabanos or chorizo), sliced
4 tomatoes, skinned, deseeded and finely chopped
¼ teaspoon dried marjoram
pinch of chilli powder (optional)
salt and freshly ground black pepper
2 tablespoons tomato purée
4 black olives, to garnish

1 Mix the sliced sausage in a bowl with the chopped tomatoes, dried marjoram and chilli powder, if using. Season to taste with salt and pepper. Spread in the prepared pastry case.
2 Add the tomato purée to one-quarter of the basic egg and milk mixture and beat vigorously with a fork until blended. Pour over the filling and bake as in basic recipe.
3 Serve warm or cold, cut into wedges. Garnish with the olives.

PRAWN AND SWEETCORN FILLING

MAKES A 20 CM/8 INCH QUICHE
100 g/4 oz peeled prawns, defrosted if frozen
200 g/7 oz can sweetcorn, drained
½ teaspoon dillweed
grated zest of ½ lemon
salt and freshly ground black pepper

TO GARNISH (optional)
fresh dill (see Buying guide)
whole prawns

1 Combine the prawns, sweetcorn, dill and lemon zest in a bowl.

Season to taste with salt and pepper. Spread in the prepared pastry case and pour over one-quarter of the basic egg and milk mixture.
2 Bake as in basic recipe. Serve warm or cold, cut into wedges and garnish with fresh dill and whole prawns, if using.

Cook's Notes

Spicy sausage and tomato filling
 TIME
Preparation 20 minutes, cooking time is 35 minutes.

● 380 calories/1600 kj per portion

Prawn and sweetcorn filling
 TIME
Preparation 15 minutes, cooking time 35 minutes.

● 320 calories/1325 kj per portion

 BUYING GUIDE
Fresh dill is available from Indian shops and good-quality greengrocers. It can also be grown very easily at home. Otherwise, dried dillweed makes a good substitute.

Pears and prunes in white wine

SERVES 8-10
350 g/12 oz large prunes
750 g/1½ lb firm dessert pears
lemon curls, to decorate (see Preparation)
whipped cream, to serve

WINE SYRUP
70 cl/1¼ pint medium dry white wine
75 g/3 oz sugar
pared zest of ½ lemon
pinch of freshly grated nutmeg

1 Cover the prunes with cold water and soak for 1 hour.
2 Meanwhile, make the wine syrup: put the wine into a saucepan with the sugar, lemon zest and nutmeg. Bring to the boil, stirring occasionally, then lower the heat, cover and simmer for 20 minutes. Strain into a clean pan.
3 Peel, quarter and core the pears over a plate to catch any juice and cut them lengthways into slices 1 cm/½ inch thick. Bring the wine syrup to the boil, add the pear slices and juice, and bring back to the boil. Simmer very gently, uncovered for 1 minute. ⚠ Using a slotted spoon, remove the pears and transfer them to the plate.
4 Drain the prunes and add them to the wine syrup. Bring to the boil and simmer, uncovered, for 4 minutes. Pour the prunes and syrup into a large serving bowl, then add the pear slices, plus any syrup and juice on the plate, and mix gently.
5 Cool, then cover and refrigerate for 24 hours.
6 To serve: remove from the refrigerator 2-3 hours before serving to take the chill off the fruit. Decorate with a sprinkling of lemon curls. Serve with a bowl of whipped cream handed separately.

Cook's Notes

TIME
Preparation, including soaking time, about 1¼ hours, plus 24 hours chilling and 2-3 hours to bring to room temperature.

PREPARATION
To make lemon curls, pare the zest from ½ lemon and cut it into long, thin sticks. Plunge into boiling water and continue to boil for 2 minutes. Drain and cover with cling film until required.

! WATCHPOINT
Do not cook the pears for more than 1 minute or they may disintegrate.

● 180 calories/750 kj per portion

Mixed fruit delight

SERVES 8-10
6 satsumas or clementines, divided into segments
350 g/12 oz green grapes, halved and deseeded (see Buying guide)
2 crisp dessert apples, cored and sliced
425 g/15 oz can black cherries, drained, halved and stoned
2-3 bananas, sliced
2-3 oz flaked almonds (optional)
whipped cream, to serve

DRESSING
6 tablespoons clear honey
6 tablespoons orange liqueur or orange juice
6 tablespoons lemon juice

1 Put all the prepared fruit into 1 large or 2 smaller serving bowls.
2 Put all the dressing ingredients into a bowl and stir until well mixed. Pour over the fruit, turning them gently with a large metal spoon until thoroughly coated.
3 Cover with cling film, then refrigerate for 2-3 hours. Before serving, remove from the refrigerator and allow to come to room temperature for at least 30 minutes. Serve decorated with flaked almonds, if wished with a bowl of whipped cream handed separately.

Cook's Notes

TIME
Preparation time 45 minutes, plus 2-3 hours chilling time and at least 30 minutes to bring to room temperature.

VARIATION
Instead of satsumas, use a 300 g/11 oz can of thoroughly drained mandarin segments.

BUYING GUIDE
Save time by choosing seedless Californian or Cypriot grapes if available.

● 230 calories/975 kj per portion

Lime ice box pudding

SERVES 10
grated zest of 2 limes
juice of 3 limes
3 eggs, separated
100 g/4 oz caster sugar
425 ml/¾ pint double cream
8 plain sweet biscuits, crushed
fresh lime slices, to decorate

1 Line the base of a 1.7 L/3 pint loaf tin with greaseproof paper.
2 Put the egg yolks in a large heatproof bowl over a pan half full of gently simmering water. Using a rotary or hand-held electric mixer, slowly whisk in the sugar until pale and thick. Remove from heat and stir in lime zest and juice.
3 Whip the cream until standing in soft peaks and fold into the lime mixture.
4 In a clean, dry bowl and using clean beaters, whisk the egg whites until standing in soft peaks. Using a large metal spoon, fold the egg whites into the lime mixture.
5 Sprinkle a thin layer of biscuit crumbs over the base of the tin. Carefully pour in the lime mixture and top with a layer of the remaining biscuit crumbs.
6 Cover with foil, then place in the freezer compartment of the refrigerator or in the freezer and freeze for about 8 hours, or overnight, until firm.
7 To serve (see Cook's tip): uncover the tin, then run a palette knife around the edges of the pudding to loosen it. Turn out on to a flat serving plate and remove the greaseproof paper. Decorate the pudding with slices of lime and serve at once.

Cook's Notes

TIME
Preparation takes 40 minutes, plus about 8 hours freezing time.

COOK'S TIP
The pudding may be unmoulded before the party begins – return the un-decorated, turned out pudding to the freezer until ready to serve. Decorate with lime at the last moment.

WATCHPOINT
Make sure that the egg yolks and sugar are really thick before removing from the heat.

FREEZING
Freeze at the end of stage 6. Overwrap and return to the freezer for up to 1 month.

●365 calories/1525 kj per portion

Family picnic

A picnic by the sea is a great way to entertain the family, as long as the food is well planned. We have devised a picnic for six that can be made in advance and is easy to serve: we suggest a savoury choice of pasties, ham rolls, drumsticks and egg pies, all of which are easy to eat with your fingers and can be neatly packed. The creams for pudding are ready-made in sandproof containers, and are accompanied by crunchy shortbread.

Tuna puff pasties

SERVES 6
2 × 200 g/7 oz cans tuna fish, drained and flaked
1 tablespoon vegetable oil
1 onion, finely chopped
3 hard-boiled eggs, chopped
2 potatoes, boiled and diced
3 tablespoons tomato ketchup
1 teaspoon dried mixed herbs
grated zest of 1 lemon
2 eggs, beaten
1 clove garlic (optional)
dash of Worcestershire sauce (optional)
salt and freshly ground black pepper
400 g/13 oz frozen puff pastry, defrosted

1 Heat the oil in a frying-pan, add the onion and fry gently for 5 minutes until soft and lightly coloured. Transfer with a slotted spoon to a bowl.
2 Add the tuna to the bowl [!] together with the hard-boiled eggs, potatoes, tomato ketchup, herbs, lemon zest, half the beaten egg, garlic and Worcestershire sauce, if using. Season with salt and pepper to taste and mix well.
3 Heat the oven to 220C/425F/Gas 7.
4 Roll out the pastry on a lightly floured surface to a 35 cm/14 inch square. Trim the edges straight, then cut the pastry in half. Cut each half in 3 crossways.
5 Spoon a portion of the tuna and egg mixture on to the centre of each piece of pastry. Brush the edges of each piece of pastry with water, then draw up the 2 long sides to meet over the filling. Firmly seal the edges together and crimp. Press the short sides together to seal them,

making a neat parcel. Repeat this process with the remaining pastry pieces.
6 Place the 6 parcels on a dampened baking sheet and brush them with the remaining beaten egg. Bake in the oven for 15-20 minutes until the pastry is golden brown and the underside is dry. Carefully transfer to a wire rack and leave to cool.

Herby chicken drumsticks

SERVES 6
6 chicken drumsticks
75 g/3 oz dried white breadcrumbs (see Preparation)
1 teaspoon dried rosemary
1 teaspoon dried thyme
1 teaspoon dried marjoram
salt and freshly ground black pepper
2 tablespoons plain flour
2 eggs, beaten
2 tablespoons milk
2 tablespoons vegetable oil
50 g/2 oz butter

1 Mix together the breadcrumbs and herbs in a bowl and season well with salt and pepper. Place the flour in a polythene bag.
2 Put the beaten eggs in a shallow bowl and stir in the milk and a drop of oil. Put the breadcrumb mixture on a plate. Shake each drumstick in the bag of flour to coat, then dip first into the egg mixture and then into the breadcrumbs.
3 Heat the oil and butter in a large frying-pan over moderate heat. When the butter foams, add the drumsticks and fry gently for about 20 minutes until cooked through and golden brown on all sides.
4 Remove the drumsticks, drain on absorbent paper and cool.

Ham rolls

SERVES 6

12 thin slices cooked ham
225 g/8 oz smooth liver pâté
3 tablespoons medium-dry sherry
2 tablespoons single cream
salt and freshly ground black pepper

1 Put the pâté in a bowl and mash it lightly with a fork.
2 Add the sherry and cream and mash well into the pâté until the mixture is smooth. Season with salt and pepper to taste.
3 Divide the mixture between the 12 slices of ham, spreading it evenly over each slice with a knife.
4 Carefully roll up each slice of ham as tightly as possible and secure with a cocktail stick.

Picnic pies

MAKES 6
**500 g/1 lb shortcrust pastry,
   defrosted if necessary**
**600 g/1¼ lb sausagemeat (see
   Buying guide)**
6 eggs, hard-boiled
1 small egg, beaten, to glaze

1 Heat the oven to 200C/400F/Gas 6.
2 Cut pastry into 12 equal pieces, roll into balls with lightly floured hands, then roll out thinly on a floured surface into circles about 12 cm/4½ inches in diameter.
3 Line 6 individual Yorkshire pudding tins (with bases about 9 cm/3½ inches in diameter) with 6 rounds of pastry, and spread 1 tablespoon sausagemeat in the base of each.
4 Cut the eggs in half lengthways and arrange 2 pieces side by side, cut side down, on top of the sausagemeat. Divide the remaining sausagemeat into 6 and spread over the top and round the sides to cover the eggs completely.
5 Dampen the edges of the remaining pastry rounds with water and place on top of the filling. Press the edges very firmly together and then, using a floured fork, press the prongs firmly around the pastry edges.
6 Brush with beaten egg, then make a hole in the centre of each pie with a skewer. ! Make a decoration around the centre of each hole by snipping the pastry into points with kitchen scissors so that the hole looks star shaped.
7 Bake above the centre of the oven for 15 minutes, then lower the heat to 180C/350F/Gas 4 and continue baking for a further 20 minutes or until golden brown and cooked through. Cool for a few minutes in the tins, then carefully remove from the tins. Serve the pies hot, or transfer to a wire rack and leave to cool completely and serve cold.

Cook's Notes

TIME
Preparation 15 minutes, cooking 35 minutes.

SERVING IDEAS
When packing these pies, interleave them with table napkins, to ensure that the pastry is not damaged during travelling.

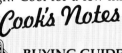
BUYING GUIDE
The more expensive types of sausagemeat are generally more meaty, but any variety is suitable for this recipe. Some sausagemeats are available with added herbs or special seasonings: these have the advantage of adding extra flavour to the pies.

! **WATCHPOINT**
The hole allows the steam to escape during the cooking time; without this hole, the shortcrust pastry is likely to crack, or the pie will split open during cooking, ruining the final result.

●875 calories/3650 kj per pie

Orange shortbread fingers

SERVES 6
100 g/4 oz plain flour
50 g/2 oz ground rice
pinch of salt
100 g/4 oz butter, softened
50 g/2 oz caster sugar
grated zest of 1 small orange
butter, for greasing
caster sugar, to decorate

1 Heat the oven to 170C/325F/Gas 3 and lightly grease a baking sheet.
2 Sift the flour, ground rice and salt on to a piece of greaseproof paper. Using a wooden spoon, beat the butter in a bowl until creamy, then beat in the sugar and orange zest until thoroughly combined.
3 Gradually work the sifted flour mixture into the butter mixture, using a wooden spoon at first and finishing by gathering the dough into a ball with your hands. !
4 Roll the dough out on a floured surface to a rectangle about 1 cm/½ inch thick, patting the shortbread into shape with your fingers to give a neat edge.
5 With a fish slice, carefully lift the shortbread on to the greased baking sheet and prick all over with a fork.

Bake in the oven for 45 minutes until lightly coloured. Immediately cut in half lengthways, then cut into fingers.
6 Cool for 10 minutes on the baking sheet until firm, then transfer to a wire rack to cool completely. Sprinkle with caster sugar if wished.

Banana creams

SERVES 6
4 bananas
400 g/14 oz can evaporated milk
2 teaspoons sugar
juice of 1 lemon

1 Slice 3 bananas and put in a blender with the evaporated milk, sugar and lemon juice. Blend until thick and smooth. Alternatively, mash the sliced bananas with a fork until they form a smooth pulp, then whisk in the remaining ingredients.
2 Divide the banana cream among 6 plastic containers (see Serving ideas) and refrigerate.
3 Just before serving, cut the remaining banana into diagonal slices and arrange on top of each portion. Serve the creams in the containers.

Buffet dinner

Why not pull out all the stops and throw a luxurious buffet dinner for twelve. Perfect for outdoor entertaining, our menu centres round a spectacular fish and vegetable salad, which is much easier to make than you might expect, and needs only a simple pasta salad accompaniment. The luscious spread finishes in style with a choice of desserts — an impressive Charlotte and a colourful fruit salad — plus irresistible rum truffles.

COUNTDOWN
The day before
● Make the fish stock, cool, cover and store in the refrigerator.
● Make the Strawberry Charlotte, but do not decorate. Refrigerate.
● Make the truffles. Refrigerate.
In the morning
● Cook the fish for the Fish and vegetable salad and mix into the mayonnaise dressing.
● Prepare and dress the vegetables for the Fish and vegetable salad.
● Make the Red fruit salad but do not decorate.
● Prepare the Pasta salad but do not add the watercress.
1½-2 hours before the party
● Decorate the Strawberry Charlotte and return to the refrigerator.
● Assemble the Fish and vegetable salad.
Just before the party
● Heat up the French bread to accompany the salad.
● Add the watercress to the Pasta salad and transfer to a serving dish.
● Sprinkle the Red fruit salad with flaked almonds.
● Remove truffles from refrigerator.

Fish and vegetable salad

SERVES 12
800 g/1¾ lb haddock fillets
1.25 L/2 pints cold water
150 ml/¼ pint dry white wine
1 bay leaf
1 onion, finely chopped
bouquet garni
6 black peppercorns
salt
500 g/1 lb French beans, cut into 5 cm/2 inch lengths
250 ml/8 fl oz oil and vinegar dressing (see Preparation)
500 g/1 lb baby carrots, cut into 5 mm/¼ inch slices
2 large green peppers, deseeded and cut into 5 cm/2 inch strips
2 large red peppers, deseeded and cut into 5 cm/2 inch strips
1 large head celery, cut into 5 mm/¼ inch slices
1 kg/2 lb unpeeled prawns
2 × 200 g/7 oz cans tuna fish
250 g/9 oz black olives

MAYONNAISE DRESSING
225 ml/8 fl oz thick bottled mayonnaise
2 teaspoons chopped fresh parsley
2 teaspoons chopped fresh dill
1 clove garlic, crushed (optional)

TO SERVE
lemon wedges
hot French bread

1 Put the water in a large saucepan together with the white wine, bay leaf, onion, bouquet garni and peppercorns. Bring to the boil then simmer for 30 minutes.
2 Strain the cooking liquid, cool and return to the rinsed-out pan. Add the haddock fillets, bring to the boil, then reduce the heat and simmer for 10 minutes or until the fish flakes easily. Remove the fish with a slotted spoon and set aside to cool. Discard the cooking liquid.
3 Rinse out the pan and fill two-thirds with cold salted water. Bring to the boil, add the French beans and boil for 5 minutes to blanch them. Remove with a slotted spoon and put into a bowl. Pour over 3 tablespoons of the oil and vinegar dressing while the beans are still warm.
4 Put the carrots into the same boiling water and cook for 3 minutes. [!] Remove with a slotted spoon, put in a separate bowl and pour over 3 tablespoons of the oil and vinegar dressing.
5 Put the pepper strips into a bowl and pour 6 tablespoons of the oil and vinegar dressing over them. Mix well. Put the celery pieces into another bowl and pour over the remaining oil and vinegar dressing.
6 Skin and flake the cooled fish fillets. Make the mayonnaise dressing: mix the mayonnaise with the chopped parsley, dill and crushed garlic, if using. Carefully

---

Cook's Notes

TIME
Preparation and cooking take 1½ hours, assembling 45 minutes.

WATCHPOINT
The timing of the vegetables is very important: they must be just blanched and not overcooked.

PREPARATION
To make the oil and vinegar dressing put 12 tablespoons olive oil, 4 tablespoons white wine vinegar, 1 teaspoon mustard and salt and freshly ground black pepper to taste in a screw-top jar. Shake well to mix.

SERVING IDEAS
This dish looks most effective if served in a fish-shaped dish. If you do not have a large platter, the salad looks very pretty piled up in a deep, straight-sided glass dish: the colours of the different layers show up beautifully.

●440 calories/1850 kj per portion

stir in the fish to coat it evenly. Set aside.

7 Reserve 14 unpeeled prawns for the garnish and peel the rest. Set aside.

8 Put the tuna fish with its oil into a large bowl and then flake it with a fork so that fish and oil are combined.

9 To assemble the salad: spread the French beans all over the surface of a large platter. Cover the French beans with a layer of carrots, leaving about 5 cm/2 inches of the beans exposed around the edge. Lightly season the celery pieces with salt and layer them on top of the carrots, leaving some carrots exposed. Cover with the pepper strips.

10 Pile the white fish mixture on top of the layer of peppers. Place the tuna fish along the top of the white fish.

11 Cover the exposed white fish mixture with the peeled prawns and arrange the unpeeled ones decoratively around the edge of the dish. Garnish with the black olives and serve with lemon wedges and hunks of hot French bread.

Pasta salad

SERVES 12
1 kg/2 lb pasta shells
salt
2 tablespoons vegetable oil
2 red dessert apples
1 large bunch spring onions, finely
  chopped
3 bunches watercress, stalks
  discarded and leaves chopped
freshly ground black pepper

DRESSING
425 ml/¾ pint thick bottled
  mayonnaise
200 ml/7 fl oz soured cream
200 ml/7 fl oz milk

1 Bring a large pan of salted water to
the boil. Add the oil, then the pasta.
Bring back to the boil, then lower
the heat slightly and simmer for
about 8 minutes or until the pasta is
just tender. [!] Drain thoroughly,
then rinse under cold running
water, to remove any excess starch.
Drain again and set aside.
2 To make the dressing: mix the
mayonnaise, soured cream and milk
together thoroughly in a large
mixing bowl.
3 Core the apples, cut into 1 cm/½
inch cubes and add to the dressing,
mixing well so that all the apple is
coated to prevent discoloration.
4 Add the spring onions and watercress to the dressing together with
the pasta. Season well with salt and
pepper, mix all the ingredients
together and set aside (see Cook's
tip).
5 Just before serving, adjust the
seasoning to taste, then pile on to a
serving dish.

Red fruit salad

SERVES 12
500 g/1 lb ogen melon, seeds
  removed (see Preparation)
75 g/3 oz light soft brown sugar
425 ml/¾ pint water
thinly pared rind of 1 lemon
4 tablespoons port
250 g/9 oz raspberries
250 g/9 oz redcurrants, stalks
  removed (see Preparation)
100 g/4 oz strawberries, hulled
500 g/1 lb black cherries, stoned
25 g/1 oz flaked almonds

1 Put the sugar, water and lemon
rind into a pan over a low heat until
the sugar has melted, then simmer
gently for 5 minutes.
2 Remove from the heat and allow
to cool. Discard the lemon rind and
stir in the port.
3 Put all the fruit into a glass serving
dish, pour over the port syrup and
chill for 2 hours.
4 Sprinkle with the flaked almonds
before serving.

Cook's Notes

Pasta salad

TIME
Preparation time is
about 15 minutes, cook-
ing time about 8 minutes.

COOK'S TIP
It is best to make the
salad at least a couple of
hours in advance to allow the
flavours to develop.

WATCHPOINT
Do not overcook the
pasta for this salad, it
should have a little 'bite' to it.

●615 calories/2575 kj per portion

Red fruit salad

TIME
Preparation time is
about 15 minutes, plus
cooling and chilling.

PREPARATION
To cut the melon
into balls, press a
melon baller firmly into the
melon flesh using a circular
action, then lift it away and
gently shake out the ball.
To remove the currants from
their stalks simply run the
prongs of a fork down a cluster.

●80 calories/325 kj per portion

Strawberry Charlotte

SERVES 12

350 g/12 oz fresh strawberries, hulled
175 g/6 oz unsalted butter, softened
100 g/4 oz caster sugar
grated zest and juice of 1 orange
¼ teaspoon almond flavouring
100 g/4 oz ground almonds
300 ml/½ pint dry white wine
450 ml/¾ pint double cream
2 packets sponge fingers
butter, for greasing

1 Grease the base of an 18 cm/7 inch deep loose-bottomed cake tin and line with greaseproof paper; grease the lining paper.

2 In a large mixing bowl, beat the butter, sugar, orange zest and almond flavouring together until light and fluffy. Gradually beat in the ground almonds alternately with 100 ml/3½ fl oz of the wine. [!]

3 Whip 300 ml/½ pint of the cream until it forms soft peaks, then fold into the almond mixture.

4 Mix the remaining wine with the orange juice in a large bowl. Trim the sponge fingers so that they are the same height as the tin. Reserve the trimmings. Dip each sponge finger quickly into the wine and orange mixture, [!] and use to line the sides of the cake tin in a single layer, placing the rounded un-trimmed end upwards and the sugar-coated side outwards.

5 Quickly soak any remaining sponge fingers, together with the reserved trimmed ends in the wine and orange mixture. Reserve 100 g/4 oz strawberries, slice the rest.

6 Spread one-third of the almond mixture over the base of the prepared tin. Cover with half the sliced strawberries and half the remaining sponge fingers and trimmed ends. Repeat these layers once more, finishing with the re-maining third of almond mixture.

7 Place a piece of greased greaseproof paper over the top. Cover with a small plate and place a weight on top to press it down.

8 Refrigerate for at least 4 hours, or preferably overnight, until the mixture is quite firm.

9 Remove the weight and paper. Place an inverted plate on top of the tin. Holding the tin and plate firmly, invert giving a sharp shake halfway round. Lift off the tin.

10 Slice all but one of the reserved strawberries. Arrange the slices over the top and around the bottom edge of the Charlotte; place the whole one in the centre. Whip the remaining cream until it forms soft peaks and pipe decoratively around the top and bottom edges. Chill until ready to serve.

Cook's Notes

TIME
Preparation takes 45 minutes, including turning out and decorating. Allow to chill for at least 4 hours or preferably overnight.

WATCHPOINT
Do not add the wine too quickly to the mixture otherwise it may curdle.
Dip the sponge fingers into the wine mixture very quickly or they will fall apart before you are able to line the tin.

DID YOU KNOW
The full name for this type of cold dessert is Charlotte russe (Russian Charlotte). It was invented in the 19th century by a great French chef and is always made with sponge fingers. There is another type of dessert with the name Charlotte: this is a moulded pudding made from layers of fruit and breadcrumbs usually served hot.

●425 calories/1775 kj per portion

Rum truffles

MAKES 36

500 g/1 lb plain dessert chocolate, broken into pieces
4 tablespoons cold, unsweetened strong black coffee
6 tablespoons double cream
4 tablespoons dark rum or brandy
40 g/1½ oz cocoa powder, for coating

1 Put the chocolate into a large heatproof bowl. Add the coffee and cream. Set the bowl over a pan of barely simmering water and leave until the chocolate has melted, stirring occasionally.
2 Remove the bowl from the pan. Using a hand-held electric whisk, whisk the chocolate mixture for 10-15 minutes, until thick enough to stand in soft peaks. Add the rum and whisk for a further 2-3 minutes.
3 Using a rubber spatula, scrape the mixture into a small bowl. Cover and refrigerate for about 1½ hours,

or until firm but not solid (see Cook's tips). Chill a baking tray.
4 Stand 36 petits fours paper cases on a baking tray. Sift the cocoa over the chilled tray.
5 Drop teaspoonfuls of the chocolate mixture on to the cocoa (see Preparation). Lightly coat your fingertips, by pressing them into

the cocoa. Shape each heap into a ball between your fingertips, then roll in the cocoa until evenly coated and place in a paper case.
6 Continue making truffles in this way until all the mixture is used. Chill for about 5 minutes to firm. Serve at room temperature (see Cook's tips).

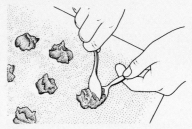

Sunday brunch

Instead of having a conventional Sunday roast, invite your friends to a casual outdoor brunch. A happy combination of breakfast and lunch, it is perfectly suited to a lazy Sunday. Served with a sparkling Champagne cocktail, you can turn it into a really special occasion.

Use your imagination freely when planning a brunch. Serve traditional breakfast fare such as bacon and eggs, as well as the savoury suggestions given here. Alternatively, make it more of a lunch party with salads and cheese. To finish on a sweet note, you can offer your friends waffles—either bought frozen or made from a packet—topped with honey or golden syrup and whipped cream or ice cream.

Smoked haddock risotto

SERVES 12
1.5 kg/3-3½ lb whole smoked haddock (see Buying guide)
1 large bunch parsley, weighing about 100 g/4 oz, stalks and tops separated
1 bay leaf
1 lemon, sliced
8 black peppercorns
100 g/4 oz butter
4 bacon rashers, rinds removed, cut into 1 cm/½ inch strips
2 onions, finely chopped
1 green pepper, deseeded and cut into thin strips
1 red pepper, deseeded and cut into thin strips
500 g/1 lb long-grain rice
4 eggs
juice of 1½ lemons
freshly ground black pepper
5 tablespoons single cream
1-2 teaspoons sweet paprika, to garnish

1 Wash the haddock and cut each fish into 3-4 pieces. Place in a large saucepan and cover with cold water. Add the stalks of the parsley, bay leaf, lemon slices and black peppercorns. Bring to the boil and simmer gently for about 10 minutes, or until the flesh flakes easily with a fork. Transfer to a plate with a fish slice and leave to cool. Strain the stock into a large measuring jug and measure 1 L/2 pints, making up the volume with water if necessary.
2 Melt half the butter in a large saucepan and fry the bacon, onions and green and red pepper strips until the onions are soft and lightly coloured. Stir in the rice.
3 Add the measured fish stock to the rice mixture and bring to the boil, stirring. Lower the heat, cover with a tight-fitting lid and simmer gently for 30 minutes, or until all the stock has been absorbed.
4 Meanwhile, remove all the skin and bones from the fish and flake the flesh. Hard-boil the eggs for 7-8 minutes, cool rapidly under cold running water, then shell and cut into quarters. Chop the parsley tops finely, reserving a few of them for garnish.
5 When the rice is cooked, gently fold in the flaked haddock, parsley, lemon juice and pepper to taste. Over low heat, fork in the cream and remaining butter until the risotto is heated all through. Transfer to a warmed serving dish and, if necessary, keep hot until ready to serve.
6 To serve: garnish with the quartered hard-boiled eggs and reserved parsley and sprinkle with a little paprika.

Cook's Notes

Smoked haddock risotto

TIME
20 minutes preparation, 50 minutes cooking.

BUYING GUIDE
If whole smoked haddock is not available, use smoked cod or haddock fillets.

●345 calories/1450 kj per portion

Devilled kidneys

SERVES 12
24 lamb kidneys, halved (see Buying guide)
100 g/4 oz margarine or butter
2 large onions, finely chopped
2 tablespoons mustard powder
2 tablespoons Worcestershire sauce
2 tablespoons mustard ketchup or 1 tablespoon tarragon vinegar mixed with 1 tablespoon dry mustard powder
pinch of cayenne pepper
salt and freshly ground black pepper
1-2 tablespoons chopped parsley

1 Melt half the margarine in a saucepan, add the onions and fry over gentle heat until just translucent.
2 In a bowl, blend the mustard powder with the Worcestershire sauce to form a smooth paste. Stir in the mustard ketchup, then add this mixture to the onions. Stir thoroughly and bring to a slow simmer. Turn down the heat and allow the mixture to simmer, uncovered, while you cook the kidneys separately.
3 Melt the remaining margarine in a large frying-pan, add the kidneys and fry over moderate heat until browned on all sides. When they are lightly browned, transfer the kidneys, with their pan juices, to a shallow flameproof dish.
4 Heat the grill to high.
5 Remove the sauce from the heat, add the cayenne and salt and pepper to taste, then pour over the kidneys. Place under the grill for 1-2 minutes until the sauce is bubbling. If necessary, keep hot until ready to serve. Sprinkle the kidneys with a little finely chopped parsley just before serving.

Cook's Notes

Devilled kidneys

TIME
Preparation 15 minutes, cooking 20 minutes.

BUYING GUIDE
Lamb kidneys may be bought fresh or frozen. If fresh they are usually sold in their natural covering of fat (suet). This should be removed before cooking and, if you wish,

can be melted down and used in place of all or part of the margarine. If you buy larger sheep kidneys, allow 15-18 and cut each half into 2-3 slices.

SERVING IDEAS
Serve on slices of hot buttered toast.

Accompany the brunch with the Champagne cocktail, Buck's fizz. Well before the party, chill

four 75 cl bottles of dry Champagne, 3.5 L/6 pints orange juice, 12 glasses and a large jug. To serve: pour the orange juice into the chilled jug. Half fill each glass with orange juice, then top up with Champagne. For economy, use a sparkling Saumur wine instead of Champagne.

●175 calories/725 kj per portion

INDOOR PARTIES
Fondue party

A fondue is just the meal to serve on a warm summer's evening, when a relaxed and informal atmosphere is the order of the day. Guests cook their own share of the meat, then dip the pieces into a choice of sauces. Serve Pear tranche as a luxurious follow up.

Fondue bourguignonne

SERVES 6
1 kg/2 lb fillet steak, trimmed of fat
and cut into small cubes
300 ml/½ pint vegetable oil, for
deep-frying

1 Divide the meat between 6 individual plates.
2 Pour the oil into a fondue pot (see Cook's tips), place over moderate heat on top of the stove and heat to 180C/350F or until a bread cube browns in 60 seconds.
3 Carefully transfer fondue pot to its burner. ⟨!⟩ Allow 1-3 minutes cooking, according to taste.

Mustard sauce

MAKES ABOUT 300 ML/½ PINT
1 tablespoon French mustard
225 ml/8 fl oz soured cream
6 tablespoons olive oil
salt and freshly ground black pepper
1 sprig or 1½ tablespoons chopped
fresh dill
pinch of sweet paprika (optional)

1 Put the soured cream into a serving bowl with the mustard and oil. Season to taste and mix well.
2 Garnish with the dill and paprika, if using, then cover and refrigerate for 30 minutes before serving.

Peanut sauce

MAKES ABOUT 300 ML/½ PINT
175 g/6 oz salted peanuts, ground
½ teaspoon chilli powder
1½ tablespoons lemon juice
1 clove garlic, crushed (optional)
3 tablespoons groundnut or
vegetable oil
10-12 tablespoons warm water
¾ teaspoon soy sauce

1 Put the peanuts in a bowl together with the chilli powder, lemon juice, garlic, if using, and 2 tablespoons of the oil. Beat together to form a paste.
2 Heat the remaining oil in a small saucepan, add the nut paste and stir well over moderate heat for 2 minutes.
3 Stir in the water and soy sauce and simmer for 5-10 minutes until the sauce is grainy in appearance and has a light film of oil on the surface. Transfer to a serving bowl, cover and keep warm until serving time. Serve warm.

Yoghurt and mint sauce

MAKES ABOUT 300 ML/½ PINT
250 g/9 oz natural yoghurt
6 tablespoons finely chopped fresh
mint
2 tablespoons olive oil
salt and freshly ground black pepper

1 Work the yoghurt, mint and oil in a blender until well mixed. If you do not have a blender, crush the mint first with a pestle and mortar, then mix into the yoghurt and oil until thoroughly blended.
2 Transfer to a serving bowl and season with salt and pepper to taste. Cover and refrigerate for 30 minutes before serving.

Tomato and garlic sauce

MAKES ABOUT 300 ML/½ PINT
400 g/14 oz can tomatoes
1 tablespoon olive oil
1 onion, finely chopped
3 garlic cloves, finely chopped
1 tablespoon finely chopped fresh
basil
1 teaspoon sugar
salt and freshly ground black pepper

1 Heat the oil in a large saucepan, add the onion and garlic and fry gently for 5 minutes until the onion is soft and lightly coloured.
2 Add the tomatoes, breaking them up with a wooden spoon, increase the heat to high and bring to the boil. Boil for 3 minutes, stirring.
3 Lower the heat and add the basil and sugar, with salt and pepper to taste. Simmer for 20 minutes until the sauce has reduced slightly and is thick. Remove from heat, cover and keep hot.
4 Just before serving, reheat, stirring constantly, then transfer to a serving bowl. Serve hot.

Cook's Notes

Fondue bourguignonne

TIME
15 minutes to prepare the meat and heat oil.

COOK'S TIPS
Use a proper fondue bourguignonne pot that comes complete with burner. Do not use a ceramic pot, since it will crack with the oil's heat.
The fondue forks are used only for cooking the meat in the oil, so provide each person with a dinner fork as well.

⟨!⟩ **WATCHPOINT**
Make sure that everyone is ready to eat before transferring the fondue pot to its burner; the oil will not be at right temperature for cooking if it is left too long.

SERVING IDEAS
Serve with salad and French bread or Crusty rolls (see page 76).

●410 calories/1725 kj per portion of meat with sauces

Mustard sauce/Yoghurt and mint sauce

TIME
5 minutes preparation, 30 minutes chilling.

Peanut sauce

TIME
About 20 minutes preparation.

Tomato and garlic sauce

TIME
5 minutes preparation, 30 minutes cooking.

Crusty rolls

MAKES 12
700 g/1½ lb strong white flour
2 teaspoons salt
25 g/1 oz lard, diced
7 g/¼ oz sachet easy-blend dried
   yeast
225 ml/8 fl oz warm milk
200 ml/7 fl oz hand-hot water
50 ml/2 fl oz single cream
   or high-cream milk, for glazing
poppy or caraway seeds (optional)
vegetable oil, for greasing

1 Sift the flour and salt into a warmed large bowl. Rub in lard then stir in the yeast. Make a well in the centre. Mix the milk with the water and pour into the well, then mix to a firm dough.
2 Turn the dough out on to a lightly floured surface and knead for 10 minutes until smooth and elastic, then form into a ball. Clean and grease the bowl. Return the dough to the bowl and turn it over to coat the surface lightly with oil. Cover the bowl with oiled polythene and leave to rise in a warm place for about 1 hour, or until the dough is doubled in bulk.
3 Grease 2 baking sheets or trays thoroughly with vegetable oil.
4 Turn the dough out on to a lightly floured surface and knead for 2 minutes, then shape into rolls and arrange on baking sheets (see Preparation). Cover with oiled polythene and leave to rise in a warm place for 30 minutes, or until doubled in size.
5 Meanwhile, heat the oven to 230C/450F/Gas 8. Place a roasting tin in bottom of oven and pour in enough boiling water to come halfway up sides (see Did you know).
6 Uncover the rolls and bake in centre and just above centre of oven for 10 minutes. Remove the tin of water. Allow steam to escape from oven. Brush top and sides of rolls with cream, then sprinkle with seeds, if using.
7 Return to the oven, swapping the sheets, for a further 10 minutes, or until the rolls are rich golden brown and shiny. Transfer to a wire rack and leave to cool completely. ✳

Cook's Notes

TIME
30 minutes preparation, 1½ hours rising, then 20 minutes baking, plus about 1 hour for cooling.

DID YOU KNOW
Creating a steamy atmosphere in the oven for the first half of baking time gives the rolls a soft crust.

FREEZING
Wrap in foil, then freeze for up to 4 months. Defrost in wrapping for 4 hours, then put in moderate oven for 10 minutes.

●255 calories/1075 kj per roll

 PREPARATION
Keep bulk of dough covered while shaping each roll as follows:

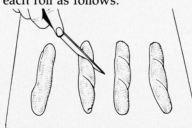

Divide the dough into 12 pieces, then roll out each to 15 × 7.5 cm/ 6 × 3 inch oval. Roll up tightly from 1 long side, then place seam side down on oiled baking sheet. Make 11 more rolls spacing well apart. Slash diagonally on top.

Pear tranche

SERVES 6
215 g/7½ oz frozen puff pastry,
  defrosted
1 small egg, beaten

PASTRY CREAM
1 egg, beaten
40 g/1½ oz caster sugar
25 g/1 oz plain flour
2 teaspoons cornflour
300 ml/½ pint milk
25 g/1 oz butter
few drops of vanilla flavouring

FRUIT FILLING
2 firm dessert pears, halved
  lengthways, peeled and cored
150 ml/¼ pint medium white wine
100 g/4 oz black grapes, halved
4 tablespoons apricot jam

1 Heat the oven to 200C/400F/Gas 6.
2 Roll out the pastry on a floured surface to a 30 × 18 cm/12 × 7 inch rectangle and make the tranche (see Preparation).

3 Prick the base with a fork, then bake in the oven for 25-30 minutes until the pastry is golden and the sides have risen. Transfer to a wire rack and leave to cool.
4 Make the fruit filling: simmer the pear halves in the white wine for about 20 minutes until tender. Leave to cool in the wine.
5 Meanwhile, make the pastry cream: place the egg in a bowl with the sugar and flours. Stir in a little of the milk to make a smooth cream.
6 Bring the remaining milk to just below boiling point, remove from the heat and gradually stir into the egg mixture. Pour back into the pan and whisk constantly over low heat until the mixture thickens and comes just to the boil. Whisk in the butter and vanilla to taste. Remove from the heat and cover with a piece of dampened greaseproof paper to prevent a skin forming. Leave until cold, then spread in the tranche.
7 Remove the pears from the wine with a slotted spoon and cut lengthways into quarters. Reserve the wine in the pan. Arrange the pear quarters crossways in a line down the centre of the pastry cream. Arrange the grapes, cut-side down,

Cook's Notes

TIME
40 minutes preparation and 25-30 minutes cooking, plus cooling time.

PREPARATION
Fold the pastry in half lengthways, then cut away a 4 cm/1½ inch border from the unfolded sides. Unfold the central piece, roll out to original rectangle, place on a dampened baking sheet and brush edges with egg. Unfold the border and lift on to the rectangle. Press the edges lightly to seal, decorate with a diamond pattern, glaze with egg

●380 calories/1595 kj per portion

in 2 lines on either side of the pears.
8 Sieve the apricot jam into 3 tablespoons of the reserved wine. Stir well over low heat until the jam has melted, then boil for 1-2 minutes until it forms a glaze.
9 Brush the fruit and pastry with the glaze and leave to set before serving.

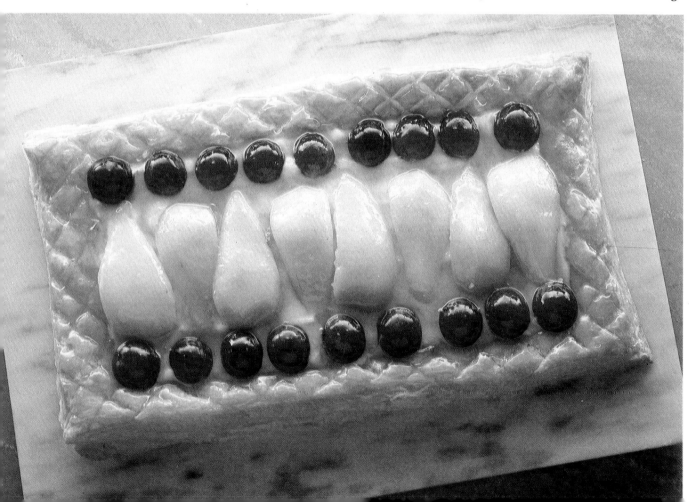

Caribbean-style dinner

The glowing, tropical mood of the Caribbean is brought into your home with this exciting menu for six. The flavours that are the very essence of West Indian cookery feature strongly in every dish. Light fish patties, spicy pork seeped in rum, a colourful salad and an exotic coconut soufflé, all add up to a truly memorable evening.

West Indian fish patties

SERVES 6
250 g/9 oz cod or haddock fillets
1 tablespoon wine vinegar
300 ml/½ pint cold water
1 tablespoon vegetable oil
½ small onion, chopped
¼ red pepper, deseeded and chopped
2 tablespoons chopped parsley
2 tablespoons canned chopped tomatoes
juice of ½ lemon
3 dashes Tabasco
salt and freshly ground black pepper
400 g/13 oz frozen puff pastry, defrosted
1 egg white, lightly beaten

1 Put the fish in a heavy pan with the vinegar and water, bring just to the boil, then lower the heat slightly and simmer gently for 10 minutes.
2 Drain the fish and, when cool enough to handle, skin, bone and flake the flesh.
3 Heat the oil in a pan, add the onion and fry gently for 5 minutes until soft and lightly coloured. Add the red pepper and parsley and cook for a further 5 minutes.
4 Add the flaked fish, together with tomatoes, lemon juice, Tabasco, 1 teaspoon salt and a generous sprinkling of pepper. Simmer, uncovered, stirring occasionally, for a further 10-12 minutes until most of the liquid has evaporated. Transfer to a bowl, taste, adjust seasoning and leave to cool.
5 Roll out the pastry on a lightly floured surface to a 40 × 30 cm/16 × 12 inch rectangle.
6 Heat the oven to 220C/425F/Gas 7.
7 Cut the pastry into twelve 10 cm/4 inch squares. Place a portion of the fish mixture in the centre of each square, then lightly dampen the pastry edges with cold water and fold each square into a triangle. Press the edges together, then crimp with a fork to seal well.
8 Arrange the patties well apart on 2 baking sheets and brush the surfaces with egg white, then prick each patty with a fork 2-3 times. Bake in the oven for about 20 minutes until the pastry is golden brown. Serve at once.

Pork roast with rum

SERVES 6
2 kg/4½ lb loin of pork on the bone
1 teaspoon salt
1 teaspoon ground ginger
½ teaspoon freshly ground black pepper

½ teaspoon ground cloves
3 cloves garlic, crushed
3 bay leaves
600 ml/1 pint chicken stock
175 ml/6 fl oz dark rum
100 g/4 oz soft brown sugar
4 tablespoons lime juice
1 tablespoon plain flour

1 Using a very sharp knife, score the skin of the pork fairly deeply, almost through to the fat, in a diamond pattern.
2 Heat the oven to 170C/325F/Gas 3.
3 Pound the salt, ginger, pepper, cloves and garlic to a paste in a mortar and pestle. Rub the paste well into the scored surface of the pork; place bay leaves on top.
4 Pour 150 ml/¼ pint of the stock into a roasting pan, together with one-third of the rum. Put the meat, skin-side up, on a rack in the pan and roast in the oven for 1 hour.
5 Meanwhile, mix the sugar, lime

Cook's Notes

West Indian fish patties

TIME
Making the fish filling, rolling out the pastry and assembling the patties takes about 1 hour, while cooking in the oven takes about 20 minutes.

●325 calories/1360 kj per patty

Pork roast with rum

TIME
15 minutes preparation, plus 2¼ hours cooking.

SERVING IDEAS
Serve with fried, sliced plantains or bananas.

●1105 calories/4640 kj per portion

juice and remaining rum in a bowl.
6 Remove the meat from the oven and baste with the sugar and lime mixture. Return the meat to the oven and continue to roast for a further 1¼ hours. Add more stock to the pan during this time, if the liquid appears to be drying out.
7 Transfer the meat to a warmed serving platter and discard the bay leaves. Keep the meat hot.
8 Pour off the liquid from the roasting pan into a jug, skim off the excess fat and return 1 tablespoon to the roasting pan. Place the pan on top of the cooker and sprinkle in the flour. Stir over low heat for 1 minute, then stir in the remaining stock and the reserved cooking liquid. Simmer, stirring constantly, until the sauce has thickened. Season to taste with salt and pepper, transfer to a warmed sauceboat and hand separately.

Carrot salad

SERVES 6
500 g/1 lb carrots
juice of 1 orange
juice of 1 lemon
50 g/2 oz desiccated coconut

1 Grate the carrots using either a hand grater or food processor (see Cook's tip). Put the grated carrots in a large bowl.
2 Mix the orange and lemon juice together, then pour over the carrots. Toss the salad well.
3 Transfer the carrots and juice to a salad bowl or divide the salad between individual serving dishes and sprinkle over the coconut.

4 Chill the carrot and coconut salad in the refrigerator for at least 1 hour or until ready to serve.

Cook's Notes

TIME
The salad takes 10 minutes to prepare, plus chilling time.

SERVING IDEAS
This refreshingly tangy salad looks particularly attractive served in coconut shells. Apart from adding bright colour to the meal, the salad provides an excellent foil to the rich pork.

COOK'S TIP
To make grating easier, crisp the carrots by soaking them whole in iced water for 1 hour before.

VARIATION
Toss the salad in an oil and vinegar dressing instead of the lemon and orange juice mixture.

● 120 calories/500 kj per portion

Coconut soufflé

SERVES 6

350 ml/12 fl oz canned coconut cream (see Buying guide)

6 eggs, separated

75 g/3 oz caster sugar

1½ rounded tablespoons (1½ sachets) gelatine

4 tablespoons cold water

2 limes (see Preparation)

90 g/3½ oz unsweetened desiccated coconut

1 Put the coconut cream into a pan and gently bring almost to simmering point. Remove from the heat and set aside.

2 Put the egg yolks and sugar in a heatproof bowl that will fit over a pan of water. Whisk together until thick and pale, then stir in the coconut cream until thoroughly mixed in.

3 Set the bowl over a pan of barely simmering water and cook, stirring constantly, for about 10 minutes until the mixture is smooth and slightly thickened. Remove the bowl from the heat.

4 Sprinkle the gelatine over the water in a heatproof bowl. Leave to soak for 5 minutes until spongy, then stand the bowl in the pan of gently simmering water for 1-2 minutes, stirring occasionally, until the gelatine has dissolved.

5 Whisk the gelatine into the coconut cream mixture, together with the lime zest and 75 g/3 oz of the desiccated coconut. Allow the mixture to cool for about 30 minutes.

6 Meanwhile, secure a paper collar around an 850 ml/1½ pint soufflé dish.

7 In a spotlessly clean, dry bowl, whisk the egg whites until they stand in stiff peaks, then fold into the cooled coconut cream mixture. Transfer to the prepared soufflé dish and refrigerate for at least 3 hours until set.

8 Meanwhile, brown the remaining desiccated coconut: put the coconut on a foil-covered grill rack and toast under a fairly hot grill for 2 minutes, turning constantly, until evenly browned.

9 Carefully remove the paper collar from the soufflé, then, using a palette knife, press the toasted coconut on to the sides. Decorate with lime slices and serve at once.

Cook's Notes

 TIME
Preparation takes 1 hour, plus 30 minutes cooling and at least 3 hours chilling.

 BUYING GUIDE
If canned coconut cream is difficult to obtain, use 115 g/4½ oz block creamed coconut dissolved in 225 ml/8 fl oz hot water.

 PREPARATION
Finely grate the zest from 1½ limes, then cut the remaining half into very thin slices for decorating.

●680 calories/2860 kj per portion

French dinner party

Remember that summer holiday in France and all the wonderful food you had? Well, now's your chance to capture the full flavour of France at home with this elegant French dinner party menu. Start with delicious scallops in vermouth and follow with a classic main course of chicken in calvados and cream, accompanied by crisp Noisette potatoes. For dessert, stun your guests with the sort of luscious creation that lures the crowds into French pâtisserie shops.

Chambéry scallops

SERVES 6
750 g/1½ lb frozen scallops (see
   Buying guide)
50 g/2 oz butter
1 onion, finely chopped
1 clove garlic, crushed
50 ml/2 fl oz Chambéry (see Buying
   guide)
1 tablespoon lemon juice
salt and freshly ground black pepper
2 tablespoons chopped fresh
   parsley
lemon twists and parsley sprigs, to
   garnish

1 Melt the butter in a large frying-pan, add the onion and garlic and fry gently for 5 minutes until the onion is soft and lightly coloured.
2 Pour in the Chambéry and lemon juice, then add the scallops and salt and pepper to taste. Stir well to mix the ingredients together.
3 Bring to the boil, then lower heat slightly, and add half the parsley. Cover and simmer gently for 15-20 minutes until the scallops are tender. [!]
4 Transfer to 6 small individual dishes, sprinkle with the remaining parsley and garnish with lemon twists and parsley sprigs. Serve.

Chicken calvados flambé

SERVES 6
1.8 kg/4 lb oven-ready chicken (see
   Buying guide)
1 tablespoon vegetable oil
50 g/2 oz butter
2 tablespoons chopped shallots
75 ml/3 fl oz calvados (see Buying
   guide)
300 ml/½ pint dry cider
salt and freshly ground black pepper
250 g/9 oz button mushrooms
150 ml/¼ pint double cream
watercress sprigs, to garnish

1 Heat the oil and butter in a large flameproof casserole, add chicken and fry it briskly, turning, until golden brown on all sides.

Cook's Notes

Chambéry scallops

TIME
This delicious starter only takes about 30 minutes to make in total.

SERVING IDEAS
Serve with chunks of hot French bread.

WATCHPOINT
Do not overcook the scallops, otherwise they will toughen.

BUYING GUIDE
Frozen scallops are available from larger supermarkets, freezer centres and high-class fishmongers.
Chambéry is a type of dry French vermouth with a mild herby flavour. If difficult to obtain, substitute another dry vermouth such as Noilly Prat.

●150 calories/625 kj per portion

Chicken calvados flambé

TIME
1½ hours to prepare and cook in total.

BUYING GUIDE
If possible, use a fresh chicken instead of a frozen one, preferably farm-raised rather than a 'mass-produced' bird – the fat will be soft and yellow, and the flesh tastier. Alternatively, try one of the maize-fed birds which are very popular in France and are now available in larger supermarkets. These birds have pale yellow flesh as a result of being fed on maize.
Calvados is an apple brandy from the region of Normandy. If you do not want to splash out on a full bottle, you may be able to find a miniature-sized bottle in an off licence. If unavailable, French brandy or armagnac are acceptable substitutes.

WATCHPOINT
Heat through only – do not allow to boil.

SERVING IDEAS
In France, vegetables are not usually served with a main course that has a sauce – to be authentic, serve them after the main course. However, if you prefer to serve vegetables with the chicken, serve them separately on individual plates – broccoli and Noisette potatoes (see page 84) would complement this dish well. Sauté potatoes make a less time-consuming alternative to Noisette potatoes.
Serve the meal with a crisp, white wine such as Muscadet.
For a change, follow the French custom of serving a green salad or a selection of cheese after the main course and before the dessert.

●685 calories/2875 kj per portion

2 Sprinkle the chicken with the shallots and remove the casserole from the heat.
3 Pour the calvados into a small pan and heat through gently. [!] Remove from heat and set alight. Pour, flaming, over chicken. Allow it to burn itself out.
4 Add the cider to the chicken, season generously with salt and pepper, then cover and return to the heat. Simmer gently for about 1 hour until the chicken is tender.
5 Meanwhile, heat the oven to 110C/225F/Gas ¼.
6 Transfer the cooked chicken to a warmed serving platter and keep hot in oven, while making sauce.
7 Add the mushrooms to cooking liquid left in the casserole and cook gently for 3 minutes. Remove the mushrooms with a slotted spoon and set aside.
8 Boil the liquid left in the casserole until it has reduced by about one-third, then return the mushrooms to the pan and stir in the cream. Heat through gently, then pour some of the sauce over the chicken and transfer the rest to a warmed sauceboat.
9 Garnish the chicken with watercress and serve at once, with the sauce handed separately.

Noisette potatoes

SERVES 6
1.5 kg/3-3½ lb potatoes (see Buying guide)
salt
75 g/3 oz butter
rosemary sprigs or fresh mint leaves, to garnish (optional)

1 Peel the potatoes and put them into a large pan of cold salted water. Leave to soak for at least 2 hours (see Cook's tips).
2 Drain the potatoes and, using a melon baller, scoop out as many balls of potato from each as possible (see Economy).
3 Bring a pan of salted water to the boil, add the potato balls and cover the pan with a lid. Bring to the boil, lower the heat and simmer gently for 4 minutes until potatoes are beginning to soften (see Cook's tips). Drain the potatoes.
4 Melt the butter in a heavy-based frying-pan. Add potato balls and fry over moderate heat, shaking pan frequently, for about 10 minutes or until the potatoes are crisp and golden on the outside but soft inside when they are pierced gently in the centre with a fine skewer.

5 Remove the potatoes from the pan with a slotted spoon and drain on absorbent paper. Transfer to a warmed dish, sprinkle with salt and serve garnished with rosemary sprigs or mint leaves, if using.

Cook's Notes

TIME
Preparation, including soaking, parboiling and cooling, is 3 hours; cooking is then only about 10 minutes.

BUYING GUIDE
Old all-purpose potatoes such as red or Desirée varieties are best for this dish.

SERVING IDEAS
Serve these potatoes as a crisp contrast to the chicken and calvados dish.

ECONOMY
Use any left-over trimmings for soups, stews and thickening sauces.

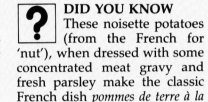
COOK'S TIPS
Soaking the potatoes before cooking helps remove excess starch which would tend to make potatoes stick together during frying.
Parboiling potatoes shortens the final cooking time and it helps produce a tender centre with a beautifully crisp shell.

? **DID YOU KNOW**
These noisette potatoes (from the French for 'nut'), when dressed with some concentrated meat gravy and fresh parsley make the classic French dish *pommes de terre à la parisienne*.

●425 calories/1775 kj per portion

Parisienne choux ring

SERVES 6
175 g/6 oz plain flour
generous pinch of salt
300 ml/½ pint water
100 g/4 oz margarine or butter
4 large eggs, lightly beaten
1 egg, beaten, to glaze
1 tablespoon blanched almonds
1 teaspoon icing sugar
vegetable oil, for greasing

FILLING
6 egg yolks
75 g/3 oz sugar
1 teaspoon vanilla flavouring
65 g/2½ oz plain flour
600 ml/1 pint milk
150 ml/¼ pint double cream,
  thickly whipped

1 Heat the oven to 220C/425F/Gas 7 and lightly grease a baking sheet.
2 Make the pastry: sift the flour and salt on to a sheet of greaseproof paper.
3 Pour the water into a large heavy-based saucepan, add the margarine and heat gently, [!] stirring occasionally, until the margarine has melted. Bring to the boil, then immediately remove from the heat and tip in the flour.

4 Stir vigorously with a wooden spoon to mix, then return to low heat and beat for about 1 minute, or until the paste forms a ball in the centre of the pan.
5 Remove from the heat and cool for a few minutes, then beat in the eggs, a little at a time. Beat until the paste is smooth and shiny.
6 Put the paste into a piping bag with a 1 cm/½ inch plain nozzle. Pipe a 25 cm/10 inch ring on to the prepared baking sheet. Pipe another ring inside, touching the first ring, then pipe a third ring on top to cover the join.
7 Carefully brush the top of the paste with the beaten egg, then sprinkle with the almonds. Bake in the oven for about 40 minutes.
8 Carefully transfer the choux ring to a wire rack and leave until cold.
9 Meanwhile, make the filling: put the egg yolks in a bowl with the sugar and vanilla, then whisk until pale and thick. Whisk in the flour.
10 Pour the milk into a pan and bring to just below boiling point. Remove from the heat and slowly stir half into the egg mixture. Stir in the remaining milk, then pour back into the pan and whisk constantly over low heat until the mixture thickens and comes to the boil. Remove from the heat and cover closely with a piece of dampened greaseproof paper to prevent a skin forming. Leave until cold.

11 To serve: slice the cold choux ring in half horizontally, then pipe or spoon the filling into the bottom half. Pipe or spoon the whipped cream on top, then replace the upper half of the choux ring. Sift icing sugar over the top and serve.

Cook's Notes

TIME
2 hours to prepare and cook, plus cooling time.

! WATCHPOINT
The water must not boil before the margarine has melted, otherwise excess evaporation will affect the balance of ingredients.

SERVING IDEAS
The French like to offer seasonal fruit with, or instead of, dessert.

? DID YOU KNOW
This is a version of the classic dessert, Paris-Brest, which is named after a bicycle race that runs in a circle from Paris to Brest (on the coast) and back to Paris. The ring of choux is meant to represent the circular course.

●635 calories/2650 kj per portion

Curry lunch

When the summer days begin to cool down, and it becomes impractical to eat outdoors, try creating your own Indian summer indoors with an imaginative curry lunch. For the main course, there's a choice of both beef and lamb curries with a vegetable curry accompaniment. The menu finishes with an exotic ice cream and a fragrant almond sweet.

COUNTDOWN
2 days before
● Marinate lamb for spiced lamb.
● Make the Indian almond sweet.
The day before
● Make the Almond and pistachio ice and freeze.
● Make the Spiced lamb.
● Make the Beef kheema without adding the peas.
40 minutes before
● Make the Vegetable curry.
15 minutes before
● Heat the Spiced lamb through.
● Heat the Beef kheema through and add the peas.
Just before the dessert
● Divide up the almond sweet.
● Unmould the ice and decorate with the nuts.

Beef kheema

SERVES 6
1.5 kg/3 lb lean minced beef
5 tablespoons vegetable oil
4 tablespoons ground coriander
3-4 tablespoons curry powder or
 garam masala (see Buying guide)
1 tablespoon ground turmeric
3 onions, finely chopped
3 cloves garlic, chopped
1 piece root ginger, 7.5 cm/3 inches
 long, peeled and chopped
2 large green peppers, deseeded and
 chopped
2 × 400 g/14 oz cans tomatoes
6 tablespoons water
350 g/12 oz frozen peas
salt

1 Heat the oil in a frying-pan, stir in the ground spices, onions, garlic and ginger and fry gently for 5 minutes until the onions are soft and lightly coloured.
2 Add the beef to the pan and fry over moderate heat until lightly browned, breaking it up with a wooden spoon. Stir in the green peppers, tomatoes with their juice and the water. Bring to the boil, then lower the heat, cover the pan and simmer for 1 hour, stirring occasionally with a wooden spoon.
3 Stir the peas into the meat, season with salt and cook for a further 15 minutes. Transfer to a warmed serving dish and serve at once.

Spiced lamb

SERVES 6

1.5 kg/3 lb boned lamb shoulder, trimmed of excess fat and cut into 1 cm/½ inch thick strips
5 tablespoons vegetable oil
20 whole black peppercorns
8 cardamom pods
4 cinnamon sticks
4 bay leaves
¼ teaspoon ground cloves
4 large onions, sliced
3 cloves garlic, chopped

MARINADE
175 g/6 oz ground almonds
2 tablespoons ground cumin
1 tablespoon ground ginger
1 teaspoon salt
500 ml/18 fl oz natural yoghurt
juice of 1 large lemon

1 Make the marinade: mix the ground almonds with the spices, salt, yoghurt and lemon juice. Put the meat in a bowl, pour over the marinade and mix well together so that the meat is well coated. Cover and refrigerate overnight.
2 Heat the oil in a large pan, add the peppercorns, cardamoms, cinnamon sticks, bay leaves and cloves and gently cook for 1-2 minutes. Add the onions and garlic and continue cooking for a further 5 minutes, until onions are soft and lightly coloured.
3 Add the meat and marinade to the pan, stir well and bring to the boil. Lower the heat, cover and simmer for 1 hour or until the meat is tender, stirring occasionally.
4 Transfer to a warmed serving dish and serve at once.

Vegetable curry

SERVES 12

6 tablespoons vegetable oil
2 tablespoons ground coriander
1 tablespoon curry powder
1 tablespoon ground turmeric
2 teaspoons ground cumin
juice of 1 large lemon
1 teaspoon salt
6 tablespoons water
750 g/1½ lb potatoes, cut into chunks
350 g/12 oz carrots, sliced
350 g/12 oz courgettes, sliced
350 g/12 oz runner beans, sliced (see Cook's tip)
6 tomatoes, quartered

1 Heat the oil in a frying-pan, add the ground spices and cook gently, stirring constantly, for 1 minute. Add lemon juice, salt and water.
2 Add the potatoes and carrots to the pan and stir well to make sure the vegetables are well covered in the curry mixture. Bring to the boil, then lower the heat, cover and simmer gently for 10 minutes.
3 Add the courgettes and beans to the pan and stir well. Continue cooking for a further 10 minutes.
4 Stir in tomatoes and cook for further 5 minutes. Transfer to a warmed serving dish; serve at once.

Cook's Notes

Beef kheema

 TIME
Preparation and cooking take 1½ hours.

 BUYING GUIDE
Curry powder is available in mild, medium and hot strengths—choose according to taste.

 DID YOU KNOW
'Kheema' is the Indian word for minced beef.

● 630 calories/2625 kj per portion

Spiced lamb

 TIME
Marinate the meat overnight, then allow about 1¼ hours to prepare and cook the dish.

 SERVING IDEAS
Serve both meat dishes with vegetable curry and boiled long-grain rice (preferably Basmati rice from northern India, considered to have the best flavour of all the long-grain rices). Other good accompaniments are a bowl of chopped onion and tomato, Raita (chopped cucumber mixed in yoghurt) and mango chutney.

● 1000 calories/4200 kj per portion

Vegetable curry

 TIME
Preparation and cooking take 40 minutes in total.

 COOK'S TIP
Use frozen beans when fresh beans are unavailable: add with the tomatoes for the last 5 minutes cooking time.

● 135 calories/575 kj per portion

Almond and pistachio ice

SERVES 12

2 tablespoons cornflour
1 L/2 pints milk
600 ml/1 pint evaporated milk
225 g/8 oz sugar
300 ml/½ pint double cream
25 g/1 oz pistachio nuts, chopped
25 g/1 oz blanched almonds, chopped
few drops of green food colouring (optional)

TO GARNISH
halved pistachio nuts
blanched almond flakes

1 Mix cornflour with 2 tablespoons of the fresh milk to make a paste, then set aside.

2 Pour the remaining milk into a saucepan, bring to just boiling point, then lower the heat and simmer over low heat, stirring, for about 10 minutes.

3 Remove from the heat and stir in the cornflour mixture, then return to the heat and bring to the boil, stirring constantly until thick and smooth. Add the evaporated milk and bring back to the boil. Add the sugar and stir until dissolved, then remove from the heat.

4 Stir in the cream, then turn the mixture into a large bowl and leave to cool, stirring occasionally to stop skin forming on surface. Stir in nuts and green food colouring, if using.

5 Pour into 2 shallow 1.25 L/2 pint freezerproof containers and freeze the mixture uncovered for about 45 minutes, or until icy around the edges and slushy in the centre.

6 Using a fork, stir the edges of the ice cream into the centre and mix lightly (see Serving ideas). Cover and freeze overnight until firm. ✳

7 To serve: dip bases of moulds quickly into hot water, then turn out and decorate with pistachio nuts and almond flakes.

Indian almond sweet

MAKES 24
100 g/4 oz self-raising flour
pinch of salt
50 g/2 oz ground almonds
50 g/2 oz semolina
50 g/2 oz margarine or butter, diced
5 tablespoons natural yoghurt
vegetable oil, for deep frying

SYRUP
350 g/12 oz sugar
425 ml/¾ pint water
3 whole cloves
1 teaspoon rose water

1 Sift the flour and salt into a bowl, then stir in the almonds and semolina. Add the margarine and rub it in until the mixture resembles fine breadcrumbs.
2 Using a round-bladed knife, gradually stir in the yoghurt. Draw together with your fingers to make a soft and moist dough.

3 Divide the dough into 24 pieces and shape each into a ball. Place in a single layer on a large baking tray and refrigerate for at least 15 minutes, to firm.
4 Meanwhile, make the syrup: put the sugar, water and cloves into a heavy-based saucepan. Heat gently, without stirring, until the sugar has dissolved, then bring to the boil and boil for 10 minutes to make a thin syrup. Remove from the heat and cool for a few minutes, then pour into a large, wide bowl and stir in the rose water. Reserve.
5 Pour enough oil into a deep-fat frier to come one-third of the way up the sides of the pan. Heat oil gently to 190C/375F or until a day-old bread cube will brown in 50 seconds.
6 Deep fry the balls of dough, in 3 batches, in the hot oil for 1-2 minutes, until deep golden brown. Drain each batch briefly on absorbent paper, then transfer to the syrup and turn with a large metal spoon until the balls are moistened on all sides. ⚠
7 Leave to cool in syrup, then cover

and refrigerate for at least 2 hours (or up to 4 days). To serve: divide between small bowls, then spoon over the remaining syrup. Serve chilled or at room temperature.

Cook's Notes

TIME
45 minutes preparation, including the frying, plus cooling and chilling time.

WATCHPOINT
Turn the almond balls very gently and with great care as they are fragile and break up easily.

DID YOU KNOW
This is an adaptation of a traditional Indian recipe, called *Gulab jamun*, which is served as a dessert. It can be decorated with chopped almonds or pistachio nuts or rose petals.

● 775 calories/3250 kj per portion

Californian-style dinner

Our informal dinner menu reflects the sunny mood and the sumptuous seafood of the west coast of the United States. The starter is a tangy mixture of avocado and crab, while the main course uses wine, tomato and garlic to bring out the flavours of prawns and white fish. To complete the meal in true American style, try Angel food cake.

Crab-stuffed avocados

SERVES 6
3 large, ripe avocados
3 tablespoons olive oil or sunflower oil
1 large onion, finely chopped
2 cloves garlic, crushed (optional)
250 g/9 oz fresh or frozen crabmeat, defrosted
2 tablespoons chopped fresh parsley
1 tablespoon red or white wine vinegar
2 dashes Tabasco
¼ teaspoon salt
¼ teaspoon freshly ground black pepper
25 g/1 oz grated Parmesan cheese

1 Heat the oil in a small, heavy-based saucepan, add the onion and garlic, if using, and fry gently for 5 minutes until soft and lightly coloured.
2 Remove the rack from the grill pan and line the base of the grill pan with foil. Heat the grill to moderate.
3 Add crabmeat to the onion, together with the parsley, vinegar, Tabasco, salt, pepper and half of the Parmesan. Increase the heat to moderate and cook for 2 minutes, stirring with a wooden spoon, to blend the flavours.
4 Cut the 3 avocados in half lengthways and remove the stones. Fill the avocado halves with crab mixture, piling it up into a mound in the centre and spreading it over the cut edges. Sprinkle the remaining Parmesan over the filled avocados.
5 Arrange the filled avocados in the grill pan and grill for about 3 minutes until the tops are browned. Serve at once.

American fish casserole

SERVES 6
1 kg/2 lb white fish fillet, skinned and cut into 5 cm/2 inch pieces (see Buying guide)
3 tablespoons olive oil or sunflower oil
2 onions, chopped
2 cloves garlic, crushed
4 spring onions, chopped
1 green pepper, deseeded and chopped
4 tablespoons chopped fresh parsley
300 ml/½ pint dry white wine
150 ml/¼ pint water
400 g/14 oz can chopped tomatoes
4 tablespoons tomato purée
25 ml/1 fl oz brandy (optional)
salt and freshly ground black pepper
100 g/4 oz peeled prawns
12 unpeeled prawns, to garnish

1 Heat the oil in a flameproof casserole, add the onions and garlic and fry over moderate heat for 10 minutes until browned.
2 Add the spring onions, green pepper and half the parsley, stir well and fry for 5 minutes.
3 Mix the wine with the water and add to the casserole, together with the chopped tomatoes, tomato purée and brandy, if using. Cook for 2 minutes to allow the alcohol to evaporate, then season to taste with salt and pepper. Add the haddock pieces and peeled prawns and stir gently to mix.
4 Cover the casserole and continue to cook over moderate heat for 15 minutes, until the haddock flakes easily. Remove from the heat, garnish with the unpeeled prawns and serve at once, straight from the casserole.

COUNTDOWN
In the morning
● Prepare the fish for the American fish casserole, cover and refrigerate.
● Make the filling for avocados.
● Make the Angel food cake.
40 minutes before
● Make the fish casserole.
● Heat the grill for the avocados.
10 minutes before
● Fill the avocados, then grill.

Cook's Notes

Crab-stuffed avocados

TIME
Preparation and cooking take about 20 minutes.

●420 calories/1750 kj per portion

American fish casserole

TIME
Preparation and cooking take about 45 minutes.

SERVING IDEAS
Serve this rich casserole with chunks of hot French bread or for a more American touch with thick slices of white bread fried in olive oil. A fresh green salad would also go well with it.

Do not forget to put out bowls for prawn shells, and napkins for wiping hands after peeling the whole prawns.

BUYING GUIDE
Any available white fish can be used here — try haddock, whiting, hake, monkfish or halibut. When in season, fresh shellfish, such as mussels and cockles, can be added at the same time as the peeled prawns. They should be cooked before adding.

●265 calories/1100 kj per portion

Angel food cake

MAKES 8-10 SLICES

50 g/2 oz plain flour
1½ tablespoons cornflour
200 g/7 oz caster sugar
¼ teaspoon salt
8 large egg whites (see Cook's tips)
¾ teaspoon cream of tartar
¼ teaspoon vanilla flavouring
¼ teaspoon almond flavouring

TO DECORATE
sifted icing sugar
225 g/8 oz strawberries

1 Heat the oven to 180C/350F/Gas 4.
2 Sift flour, cornflour, 40 g/1½ oz of the sugar, and the salt together 6 times into a bowl (see Cook's tips).
3 Sift the remaining sugar separately into a bowl.
4 Using a hand-held electric whisk, whisk egg whites at low speed in a large bowl until foamy (see Cook's tips). Add the cream of tartar and whisk, increasing the speed, until the meringue is standing in soft peaks. Using a large metal spoon, gently fold in the vanilla and almond flavourings.
5 Whisk in the sifted sugar, 1 tablespoon at a time (see Cook's tips), until the meringue is glossy and standing in stiff peaks.
6 Sift one-quarter of the sifted flour and sugar mixture evenly over the bowl, lifting the sieve high above the bowl to incorporate as much air as possible. Using a large metal spoon, quickly and lightly fold in the flour and sugar mixture, using the sides of the spoon to cut through the mixture in a figure-of-eight movement.
7 Repeat with the remaining flour and sugar mixture in 3 separate batches turning the bowl to distribute the flour and sugar mixture evenly, until all is incorporated (see Cook's tips).
8 Very gently and lightly spoon the mixture into a clean 2.25 L/4 pint tube tin or deep-sided ring tin, or 21 cm/8½ inch funnelled spring-form tin. Lightly draw a palette knife through mixture to eliminate any bubbles and pockets of air then tap the filled ring tin once vigorously against the work surface to make sure of this. Level the surface of the cake.
9 Bake in the lower part of the oven for about 40 minutes, until the top is golden, any cracks are dry, and the top springs back when pressed lightly near the centre. If any impression of your fingers remains, return the cake to the oven for a few minutes longer.
10 Invert the cake tin over a wire rack and leave the cake to cool in the tin for at least 1 hour until completely cold.
11 Loosen the sides of the cake with a thin sharp knife, then invert tin on to a plate or wire rack, and hit the sides of the tin sharply with the heel of your hand; repeat this action, several times if necessary, to unmould it. Carefully lift away the tin.
12 To decorate: dredge the cake with sifted icing sugar, then carefully transfer to a serving plate. Fill centre with strawberries and serve.

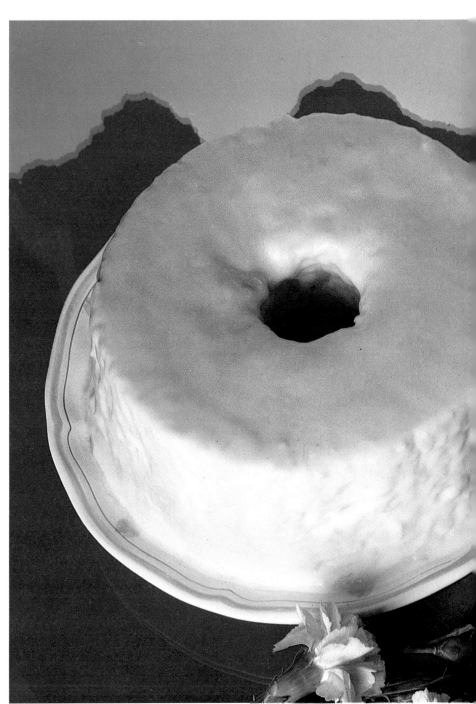

Cook's Notes

TIME
Preparation takes 30-40 minutes, baking about 40 minutes. Allow at least 1 hour for cooling.

COOK'S TIPS
Remove the eggs from the refrigerator at least 1 hour before using.

Sifting the flour and sugar 6 times is *essential* to aerate the ingredients and make sure they are thoroughly blended.

Use a scrupulously clean and dry china bowl. Avoid plastic which tends to retain grease.

Make sure the sugar is well incorporated before the next addition is made.

The flour must be folded in as quickly and lightly as possible to avoid losing the air in the mixture. Never beat or stir it in.

The cake tin must be absolutely clean, otherwise the cake will not rise.

VARIATION
Cover the cake with glacé icing instead.

● 145 calories/600 kj per slice

SALADS

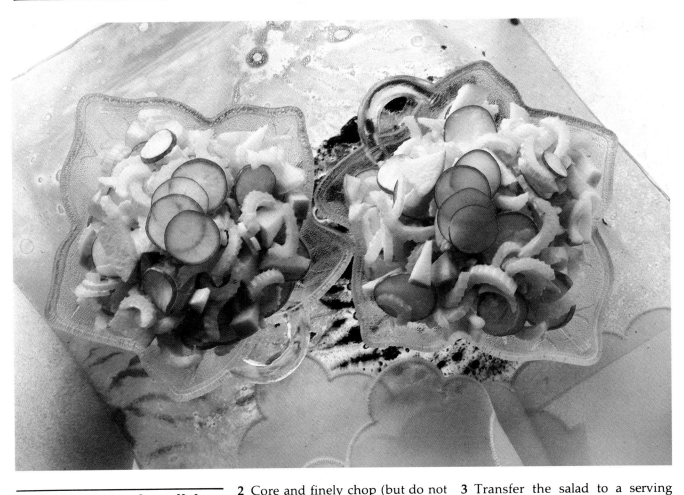

Celery and radish salad

SERVES 4
1 crisp dessert apple
1 small head celery, finely chopped
250 g/9 oz radishes, thinly sliced
  (see Buying guide)
salt and freshly ground black pepper

DRESSING
50 g/2 oz curd cheese
4 tablespoons soured cream
2 tablespoons cider vinegar
1 teaspoon light soft brown sugar
1 clove garlic, crushed (optional)

1 Make the dressing: put the curd cheese into a large bowl and beat until softened. Gradually beat in the soured cream and vinegar, then the sugar and garlic, if using.

2 Core and finely chop (but do not peel) the apple. Add to the dressing with the celery and half the radishes and mix well, adding salt and pepper to taste.

3 Transfer the salad to a serving bowl and arrange the remaining radishes on top in an attractive pattern. Serve as soon as possible, at room temperature.

Cook's Notes

TIME
Preparation takes 25 minutes.

VARIATIONS
Cream cheese may be used instead of curd cheese, and natural yoghurt instead of soured cream.

BUYING GUIDE
The average bunch of radishes available from greengrocers weighs about 100 g/4 oz, so you will need 2 bunches for this recipe.

SERVING IDEAS
This salad goes perfectly with a quiche for lunch, or with cold chicken or turkey. It also makes an attractive starter salad as shown in the photograph, served with Melba toast and butter.

DID YOU KNOW
Celery is rich in mineral salts, vitamins and iron, and is one of the best vegetables for slimmers.

●70 calories/300 kj per portion

Tropicana salad

SERVES 4-6
75 g/3 oz pasta shapes
2 grapefruits, peeled and segmented
2 oranges, peeled and segmented
2 large dessert apples, diced
3 celery stalks, finely chopped
100 g/4 oz salami, skinned and
  roughly chopped
1 tablespoon snipped chives
25 g/1 oz salted cashew nuts

DRESSING
4 tablespoons thick bottled
  mayonnaise
2 tablespoons fresh orange juice
finely grated zest and juice of 1
  lemon
2 tablespoons rosehip syrup
salt and freshly ground black pepper

TO GARNISH
slices of unpeeled orange
watercress

1 Bring a pan of salted water to the
boil and cook the pasta for about 10
minutes or until just tender. Rinse
in cold water and drain well.
2 Turn the pasta into a large bowl
and stir in the prepared fruit, celery
and salami. Mix thoroughly.
3 To make the dressing: mix
together the mayonnaise, orange
juice, lemon zest and juice and the
rosehip syrup. Whisk with a fork
until thoroughly combined. Season
with salt and pepper.
4 Toss the salad and dressing well
together, then turn into a salad bowl
and sprinkle over the chives and
cashews.
5 Serve garnished with slices of
unpeeled orange and watercress.

Cook's Notes

TIME
Preparation of this salad
takes 20 minutes plus 10
minutes to cook the pasta.

SERVING IDEAS
This makes a refreshing
and summery starter.

●430 calories/1800 kj per portion

Cucumber and strawberry salad

SERVES 4

½ cucumber, peeled and thinly sliced
100 g/4 oz strawberries, thinly sliced lengthways (see Buying guide and Cook's tips)
sprigs of fennel leaves, to garnish

DRESSING

1 tablespoon olive oil
1 tablespoon white wine vinegar
1 teaspoon caster sugar
salt and freshly ground black pepper

1 Spread the cucumber out on a plate, sprinkle with salt and leave to stand for 30 minutes (see Cook's tips). Drain and pat dry.

2 Arrange alternate circles of cucumber and strawberries on a flat, round serving plate. ⚠
3 Make the dressing: put all the dressing ingredients in a screw-top jar with a generous seasoning of salt and pepper. Shake to mix well.
4 Spoon the dressing over the salad, garnish with fennel leaves and serve at once.

Cook's Notes

 TIME
15 minutes to prepare but allow 30 minutes for salting the cucumber.

 BUYING GUIDE
Choose medium-sized strawberries which are ripe but still firm.

! **WATCHPOINT**
This salad cannot be made in advance as the strawberries will discolour the cucumber badly.

 COOK'S TIPS
If you prefer a more decorative effect, do not hull the strawberries before you slice them.
The salt draws out excess moisture from the cucumber so finished dish is not too watery.

 SERVING IDEAS
Serve with cold chicken or poached fish for a colourful accompaniment.

●45 calories/200 kj per portion

Fresh asparagus with egg dressing

SERVES 4
500 g/1 lb fresh slender
    asparagus spears
salt

CHOPPED EGG DRESSING
2 teaspoons lemon juice
1 tablespoon white wine vinegar
5 tablespoons olive oil
¼ teaspoon salt
freshly ground black pepper
¼ teaspoon mustard powder
1 teaspoon capers, chopped
1 teaspoon finely chopped parsley
1 teaspoon snipped chives
1 hard-boiled egg, finely chopped

1 Wash the asparagus stalks well in cold water, then trim the base of each spear, leaving 2 cm/¾ inch of the harder white stem. Make sure that the asparagus spears are trimmed to an even length, then divide into 4 separate bundles.

2 Tie each bundle securely with string in 2 places: just below the tips and towards the base.

3 Half-fill a deep narrow saucepan with lightly salted water and bring to the boil. Remove from the heat and stand the bundles of asparagus upright in the pan with the tips extending out of the water so that they cook in steam (see Cook's tip).

4 Cover the pan with foil to make a domed lid high enough to cover the asparagus without crushing the tips. Tuck the foil securely around the rim of the pan.

5 Return the pan to the heat, bring to the boil and boil gently for about 20 minutes, or until the thick part of the stem feels tender when pierced with a sharp knife.

6 Lift out the asparagus very carefully with kitchen tongs, then drain on absorbent paper. Lay on a clean, folded tea-towel and leave for at least 2 hours until cold.

7 Meanwhile, make the dressing: put all the ingredients in a screw-top jar and shake briskly.

8 Cut the strings around the asparagus with kitchen scissors, then arrange the cold spears on 4 individual plates. Pour dressing over each portion and serve at once.

Cook's Notes

TIME
15 minutes preparation; about 20 minutes cooking the asparagus, plus at least 2 hours cooling time.

SERVING IDEAS
Serve as a starter for a special dinner, or as a light meal with crusty bread rolls and butter.

COOK'S TIP
If the pan is too wide to allow the asparagus to stand up firmly, place a jam jar filled with hot water in centre of pan and arrange asparagus around this. Add boiling water to half-fill pan, season with salt, continue as described.

● 190 calories/800 kj per portion

Apple coleslaw

SERVES 4
350 g/12 oz white cabbage
2 dessert apples (see Cook's tip)
3 tablespoons lemon juice
2 carrots
150 g/5 oz thick bottled mayonnaise
salt and freshly ground black pepper

1 Shred the cabbage finely with a sharp knife, discarding the central core. Put the shredded cabbage into a large bowl.
2 Coarsely grate the apples without peeling them. Sprinkle the grated apples with 2 tablespoons of the lemon juice in order to prevent the flesh from discolouring.

3 Scrape the carrots, then grate coarsely. Add the apple and carrots to the cabbage and toss well.
4 Mix the mayonnaise with the remaining lemon juice and salt and pepper to taste. Add to the cabbage mixture, toss thoroughly to combine then transfer to a dish.

Cook's Notes

TIME
This coleslaw only takes about 15 minutes to prepare.

VARIATIONS
For a coleslaw that is lighter in flavour as well as calories, replace the mayonnaise with 150 ml/¼ pint soured cream and 2 tablespoons milk. Cheese can be added for flavour; use about 50 g/2 oz of coarsely grated Cheddar or Gruyère.

SERVING IDEAS
Coleslaw is the perfect accompaniment to sliced cold meats, or cold pies and flans. Garnish with sliced apples.

COOK'S TIP
Coleslaw can be made several hours in advance, omitting the grated apple. Add the apple to the coleslaw and toss the salad just before serving.

●305 calories/1275 kj per portion

Tomato and Mozzarella salad

SERVES 6

500 g/1 lb firm ripe tomatoes, cut
    into 5 mm/¼ inch slices
2 tablespoons chopped fresh
    parsley
2 tablespoons chopped fresh basil
    or ½ teaspoon dried basil
pinch of sugar
salt and freshly ground black pepper
175 g/6 oz Mozzarella cheese, cut
    into 5 mm/¼ inch slices (see Did
    you know)
3 tablespoons black olives
4 tablespoons olive oil

1 Arrange the tomato slices in an
overlapping circular pattern around
a flat serving dish. Sprinkle over the
herbs and sugar and season with
salt and pepper to taste. Cover the
dish loosely with foil and chill in the
refrigerator for 30 minutes.
2 Remove the foil and arrange the
cheese slices in the centre of the
tomatoes. Scatter the olives over.
3 Just before serving, pour over the
olive oil and, using a fork, gently lift
up the tomato slices so that the oil
drains through to them. Serve at
once.

Cook's Notes

TIME
Total preparation and
chilling time is 45
minutes.

DID YOU KNOW
Mozzarella cheese
comes from southern
Italy. Originally made from
buffalo milk, but nowadays
usually made with cow's milk, it
is mild and moist, with a very
definite flavour. It is available
from most delicatessens.

SERVING IDEAS
This classic Italian
tomato salad, which is
dressed with oil alone, and not
the more usual oil and vinegar
dressing, makes a good accompaniment to roast and grilled
meats. Serve it with pork chops
or steak or, for a change, with
roast or grilled chicken. Well
chilled, it also makes a refreshing,
easy-to-prepare first course.

●205 calories/850 kj per portion

Potato and pepper salad

SERVES 4-6
500 g/1 lb small new potatoes,
 scrubbed
1 green pepper
salt
2 celery stalks, diced
1 onion, finely chopped
½ cucumber, peeled and diced
celery leaves, to garnish

DRESSING
150 ml/¼ pint soured cream
1 teaspoon French mustard
pinch of cayenne

1 Cook the potatoes in boiling
salted water for about 15 minutes,
until just cooked. Drain and leave to
cool completely.
2 Deseed the green pepper, slice off

Cook's Notes

 TIME
30 minutes to make,
plus cooling time.

 VARIATIONS
As a quick alternative,
use drained canned
new potatoes.
 To give the dressing a milder
flavour, use American mustard
instead of French.
 To serve the salad as a light
supper dish, add 100 g/4 oz
chopped ham at stage 3.

 SERVING IDEAS
This tasty salad is a
good accompaniment to
grilled or barbecued steaks,
lamb chops or chicken.

 COOK'S TIP
For convenience, all
the vegetables may be
prepared a few hours ahead –
cover the bowl and refrigerate
until required.

●190 calories/800 kj per portion

a few rings and reserve for the
garnish. Dice the rest of the pepper.
3 Combine green pepper, celery,
onion and cucumber in a salad
bowl. Cut the potatoes in half and
add them to the salad bowl of
vegetables (see Cook's tip).
4 Just before serving, make

dressing: put the cream in a bowl
with the mustard, cayenne and
1 teaspoon salt. Mix well.
5 Pour the dressing over the salad
and toss together. Garnish the salad
with the reserved pepper rings and
a few celery leaves and serve at
once.

Oasis salad

SERVES 4
250 g/9 oz red cabbage, shredded
75 g/3 oz stoned dates, roughly
    chopped
50 g/2 oz shelled hazelnuts,
    roughly chopped
2 celery stalks, thinly sliced
2 dessert apples
1 orange, thinly sliced, to garnish

DRESSING
3 tablespoons vegetable oil
2 tablespoons orange juice
1 teaspoon finely grated orange
    zest
salt and freshly ground black pepper

1 In a salad bowl, mix together the
shredded cabbage, dates, hazelnuts
and sliced celery.
2 Make the dressing: combine the
oil in a separate bowl with the
orange juice and zest. Season to
taste with salt and pepper and mix
to combine well.
3 Quarter and core the apples, but
do not peel them. Slice them
straight into the orange dressing to
preserve the colour of the fruit.
4 Turn the apples and dressing into
the salad bowl and toss to mix
thoroughly with other ingredients.
5 Garnish the salad with the orange
slices and serve at once.

Cook's Notes

TIME
This salad takes only
15 minutes to make.

SERVING IDEAS
Crisp and colourful,
this mixed vegetable,
fruit and nut salad goes very
well with cold poultry and
meats, especially duck or pork.

VARIATION
Serve the salad as a first
course, piled into a dish
lined with lettuce or spinach
leaves and accompanied by hot
crusty French bread.

●240 calories/1000 kj per portion

minutes or until just tender. Drain well and mix with the potatoes in a bowl. While the vegetables are still warm, pour over 2 tablespoons of the marinade from the beef and gently turn them with a fork, without breaking them up, to coat thoroughly with the marinade. Cover and chill in the refrigerator for 1 hour.

6 When ready to serve, mix the grated carrots and the tomatoes with the potatoes and beans. Remove the meat slices from the marinade, draining off any excess marinade from the slices. Remove the onions from the marinade with a slotted spoon and mix them into the mixed vegetables.

7 Pile the vegetable salad into the centre of a serving platter and arrange the marinated beef slices around it. Garnish the platter with black olives and chopped parsley. Serve at once.

Cook's Notes

TIME
Cooking the beef takes about 1 hour. Allow 5-6 hours or overnight for marinating the beef. Preparing the vegetable salad, including cooking the potatoes and beans, takes about 30 minutes. Allow 1 hour for chilling the salad.

BUYING GUIDE
Most supermarkets have a selection of beef roasting joints. Choose one that is lean and without gristle. Rolled topside would be a good choice for this dish, or boned rolled fore rib, which is slightly less expensive.

COOK'S TIP
How long you cook the beef depends on whether you like it rare or well done, but this dish is most attractive if the meat is still pink. A joint of this weight will be just turning from pink after 1 hour's cooking. Cook for only 50 minutes if you like your beef rare, and for 1¼ hours if you like a joint to be well done.

●440 calories/1825 kj per portion

Marinated summer beef

SERVES 4

750 g-1 kg/1½-2 lb beef roasting joint (see Buying guide)
100 ml/3½ fl oz vegetable oil
150 ml/¼ pint dry white wine
1 teaspoon mild French mustard
1 teaspoon dried thyme
1 tablespoon lemon juice
1 clove garlic, crushed (optional)
salt and freshly ground black pepper
1 small onion, finely sliced

SALAD

2 potatoes
100 g/4 oz French beans, fresh or frozen
2 carrots, grated
2 tomatoes, quartered

GARNISH

8-10 black olives
1 tablespoon chopped fresh parsley

1 Heat the oven to 180C/350F/Gas 4.
2 Wrap the beef in foil and place in a roasting tin. Roast in the oven for about 1 hour (see Cook's tip). Remove from the oven and leave the beef, still wrapped in foil, to cool for about 45 minutes.
3 Make the marinade: put the oil, wine, mustard, thyme, lemon juice and garlic, if using, in a bowl or in the goblet of a blender. Season with salt and pepper and beat well with a fork, or process in the blender for 30 seconds.
4 Slice the cooled beef into even, neat slices and arrange them in a shallow dish. Arrange the onion slices on top of the beef and pour over the marinade. Cover the dish of beef with cling film and refrigerate for at least 5-6 hours or overnight if possible.
5 Make the salad: cook the potatoes in boiling salted water for 15-20 minutes or until just tender. Drain, cool slightly and cut into bite-sized chunks. Meanwhile, cook the beans in boiling salted water for 5-10

Summer ham salad

SERVES 4
175 g/6 oz long-grain rice
225 g/8 oz cooked lean ham, diced (see Buying guide)
225 g/8 oz can pineapple cubes, drained, or 4 slices fresh pineapple, cored and chopped
25 g/1 oz unsalted peanuts or walnut pieces
200 g/7 oz can sweetcorn kernels, drained
2 spring onions, chopped
1 small green pepper, deseeded and diced
salt and freshly ground black pepper

DRESSING
2 teaspoons French mustard
1 clove garlic, crushed (optional)
150 ml/¼ pint soured cream or natural yoghurt
1 teaspoon snipped chives, spring onion tops or finely chopped fresh parsley

TO GARNISH
lettuce leaves
1 large tomato, cut into eighths
black olives

1 Bring a large saucepan of salted water to the boil, add the rice and cook for about 12 minutes or until tender. Rinse well under cold running water, to ensure that the grains remain separate and the rice cools quickly, then drain and put into a large bowl.
2 Add the ham, pineapple, peanuts, sweetcorn, spring onions and green pepper to the rice. Stir all the ingredients together with a fork. Season the salad lightly with salt and pepper.
3 Make the dressing: in a small bowl, blend the mustard and garlic, if using, with the soured cream. Stir in the chives. Spoon the dressing into the salad and stir lightly but thoroughly, making sure that all the ingredients are evenly coated with dressing.
4 Line a serving dish with lettuce leaves. Pile the salad on to the dish and garnish with tomato wedges and olives. Refrigerate for about 15 minutes, then serve.

Cook's Notes

TIME
Preparation, including cooking the rice and making the dressing, takes about 30 minutes. Allow 15 minutes chilling time.

VARIATION
Chinese leaves may be used instead of lettuce leaves, for garnish. Orange and cashew nuts can be used instead of pineapple and peanuts.

SERVING IDEAS
Serve with hot garlic or herb bread.

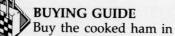
BUYING GUIDE
Buy the cooked ham in a whole piece from the delicatessen counter of the supermarket; ready sliced ham would not give a sufficiently chunky texture.

●450 calories/1900 kj per portion

Sweet and sour turkey salad

SERVES 4

350-500 g/12 oz-1 lb cooked turkey, cut into bite-sized pieces

430 g/15¼ oz can pineapple bits in natural juice, drained with juice reserved, cut into small pieces

150 g/5 oz small mixed pickles (see Buying guide)

100 g/4 oz fresh beansprouts (see Buying guide)

250 g/9 oz hard white cabbage, finely shredded

100 g/4 oz carrots, coarsely grated

50 g/2 oz dry roasted peanuts

2 tablespoons sesame seeds, lightly toasted

1 bunch watercress

4 firm tomatoes, sliced

DRESSING

2 tablespoons reserved canned pineapple juice

3 tablespoons vegetable oil

good pinch of salt

pinch of mustard powder

pinch of paprika pepper

1-2 teaspoons soy sauce

1 Mix the turkey together with the pineapple, pickles, beansprouts, cabbage, carrots and peanuts.

2 Make the dressing: place the ingredients in a screw-top jar and shake them well together.

3 Pour the dressing over the prepared salad and mix thoroughly.

4 Pile the salad into the centre of a serving platter and sprinkle with sesame seeds. Surround with a border of small sprigs of watercress and sliced tomatoes. Serve at once.

Chicken, fruit and nut salad

SERVES 4
250 g/9 oz cooked chicken, cut into bite-sized pieces
2 small dessert apples
100 g/4 oz green grapes, halved and deseeded
40 g/1½ oz shelled walnuts, chopped
2 heads chicory (see Buying guide)

HONEY DRESSING
2 tablespoons thick honey
4 tablespoons lemon juice
4 tablespoons vegetable oil
¼ teaspoon dried tarragon
salt and freshly ground black pepper

1 Make the dressing: put the honey, lemon juice, oil and tarragon into a large bowl and season with salt and pepper to taste. Whisk together until all the ingredients are smoothly blended.
2 Peel, core and chop the apples (see Cook's tip). Mix them into the dressing with the chicken, grapes and walnuts. Stir well to coat all the ingredients with dressing. Cover and allow to stand for up to 20 minutes for the flavours of the salad to combine.
3 Using a small, sharp knife, trim the chicory leaves of any brown edges and cut a thin slice from the base of each head. Cut the heads in half and remove the hard core. Wash the chicory under cold running water and drain well, then pat dry with absorbent paper.
4 Arrange some of the chicory leaves around the edge of a serving dish. Cut up any remaining chicory, mix into the salad and pile it in the centre of the dish. Serve the salad at once.

Cook's Notes

TIME
Preparation takes about 20 minutes, then allow to stand for 20 minutes.

BUYING GUIDE
Chicory bruises easily, so choose it carefully. It is sold by weight, but you can choose by size. An average head weighs about 150 g/5 oz.

SERVING IDEAS
Serve the salad with small boiled potatoes sprinkled with chopped parsley.

COOK'S TIP
It is not essential to peel the apples: the green skin of a Granny Smith or the red skin of a Red Delicious looks attractive in the salad.

●335 calories/1400 kj per portion

Melon fruit salads

SERVES 4
2 small melons (see Buying guide)
1 mango, thickly sliced and cut into cubes
300 g/ 11 oz can mandarin orange segments, drained
1 tablespoon frozen concentrated orange juice, defrosted
250 g/9 oz raspberries, hulled
caster sugar and double cream, to serve

1 Prepare the melons (see Preparation), reserving all of the trimmings. Wrap the melons in polythene bags, seal [!] and chill until required.

2 Trim the flesh from the melon trimmings and place in a bowl with the mango. Add the mandarin segments and orange juice and stir the fruits gently to mix. Cover the bowl with cling film and chill in the refrigerator for at least 1 hour.

3 To assemble: drain any juice from the melons, then place them on 4 dessert plates. Drain the other fruits well, then gently stir in the raspberries. [!] Pile the mixture into the melons. Leave to stand at room temperature for a few minutes before serving to take the chill off. Hand a bowl of caster sugar and a jug of cream separately.

Cook's Notes

TIME
40 minutes preparation, plus at least 1 hour chilling time.

BUYING GUIDE
Charentais or small cantaloupe melons are the perfect size for this dessert, and their sweet, orangy-coloured flesh blends beautifully with the other fruits. If neither is available, use green-fleshed ogen melons instead.

Ripe melons feel heavy for their size and the end opposite the stalk will 'give' slightly if gently pressed. At their peak, charentais and cantaloupe melons have a strong, musky scent.

PREPARATION
Small melons make attractive edible containers for fruit salads. (The melon flesh is eaten when the filling is finished.) To prepare: trim off the stalk, then cut the melons horizontally in half. Scrape out the seeds and membrane. Cut small 'V'-shaped wedges around the cut edges of each melon half to give a waterlily effect. Drain any juice from the cavity.

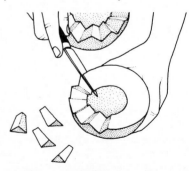

WATCHPOINTS
Once cut, melon must be tightly wrapped or its scent will permeate other foods in the refrigerator.

Do not add the raspberries until ready to assemble the salad, or their colour will run and spoil its appearance.

●155 calories/650 kj per portion

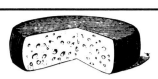

Gingered fruit cocktails

SERVES 4

3 unpeeled dessert apples, cored and sliced

2 large oranges, peeled and chopped, with pips removed (see Preparation)

½ small melon, peeled, seeded and cubed (see Buying guide)

2 tablespoons light soft brown sugar (optional)

150 ml/¼ pint soured cream

8-10 gingernut biscuits, coarsely crushed

1 Place the prepared fruit in a heavy-based saucepan. Cover and cook gently until the apples and melon are tender but not mushy. Remove from the heat. Taste the fruit mixture and sweeten with brown sugar, if necessary, ⚠ then leave to cool.

2 Divide fruit mixture between 4 dessert glasses. Cover each glass with cling film and refrigerate for 20-30 minutes.

3 To serve: spoon the soured cream over the fruit and sprinkle the crushed biscuits on top. ⚠

DRINKS PARTIES

Wine and cheese party

A casual wine and cheese party is the perfect way to entertain during warm summer days – the pace is relaxed, the food light-weight and, best of all, the preparation is minimal, leaving you cool and unflustered to enjoy the company of your friends. To ring the changes, we suggest that you serve a fruity wine punch instead of just wine, and, in addition to a plain cheeseboard, why not surprise guests with a tray of cheesy nibbles and a dip with biscuits.

Fruity red wine punch

FILLS 60 × 125 ML/4 FL OZ GLASSES
3 L/5 pints red wine (see Buying guide)
½ bottle brandy
1 green apple
1 red apple
2 pears
3 L/5 pints lemonade, chilled
ice cubes

1 Pour the wine and brandy into a large bowl and stir with a long-handled spoon to mix well.
2 Cut the green apple into quarters, remove the core, then slice and add to the wine and brandy. Slice the red apple and pears in the same way and add to the bowl. Leave to soak for at least 1 hour to allow the flavours to amalgamate.
3 Pour in the chilled lemonade and add the ice just before serving. To serve: ladle the punch into a jug.

Horseradish cheese dip

SERVES 12
500 g/1 lb curd cheese
2 × 150 ml/¼ pint cartons soured cream
6 tablespoons horseradish sauce
2 tablespoons redcurrant jelly
salt and freshly ground black pepper
small savoury biscuits, to serve

1 Put the cheese in a bowl and mash lightly with a wooden spoon, then beat in the soured cream and horseradish until evenly blended (see Cook's tip).
2 Melt the redcurrant jelly in a small saucepan over gentle heat. Allow to cool for 2 minutes, then stir into the cheese mixture.
3 Season to taste with salt and pepper and turn into a small serving bowl. Refrigerate until needed, then serve with small savoury biscuits.

Cheese nibbles

MAKES 40-50
350 g/12 oz full-fat soft cheese, chilled
175 g/6 oz finely chopped mixed nuts
20-25 green olives, stuffed with pimientos

1 Spread the finely chopped nuts out on a plate.
2 Take a teaspoonful of the cheese and shape it with your fingers round an olive to completely enclose the olive. Roll the cheese-coated olive in the nuts until lightly coated and transfer to a large plate.
3 Coat the remaining olives in the same way and refrigerate.
4 Just before serving, cut each ball in half with a sharp knife and arrange, cut-side upwards, on a serving platter. Serve as a nibble accompanied by cocktail sticks for ease in picking up.

Cheese and caraway biscuits

MAKES ABOUT 20
100 g/4 oz plain flour
¼ teaspoon celery salt
good pinch of dry mustard
50 g/2 oz butter, diced
1 tablespoon grated Parmesan cheese
¼ teaspoon caraway seeds
1 egg yolk
1½ tablespoons water
margarine, for greasing

1 Heat the oven to 190C/375F/Gas 5 and grease 2 baking sheets with the margarine.
2 Sift the flour, celery salt and mustard into a bowl. Rub in the butter until the mixture resembles fine breadcrumbs. Stir in the cheese and caraway seeds.
3 Mix the egg yolk with the water, then stir into the flour mixture. Bind together to make a stiff dough.
4 Turn the dough out on to a lightly floured surface and knead gently until smooth. Wrap in cling film or foil and refrigerate for 30 minutes.
5 Roll out the pastry very thinly on a lightly floured surface and cut into rounds with a 5 cm/2 inch fluted cutter. Transfer to baking sheets.
6 Bake in the oven for 5 minutes, then swap the sheets around and continue to bake for 5 minutes until crisp and pale golden. Remove from the oven, allow to settle for 1-2 minutes, then transfer to a wire rack and leave until completely cold.

Tropical evening

Temperatures will soar with these three knockout tropical cocktails! Full of Caribbean flavour and served icy cold, these drinks are great for serving on a sweltering day. Exotic coconut slices complete the tropical atmosphere.

Caribbean blues

MAKES 6 SHORT DRINKS
350 ml/12 fl oz vodka
75 ml/3 fl oz blue Curaçao
75 ml/3 fl oz dry vermouth
plenty of crushed ice, to serve

1 Put all the ingredients, except the ice, in a large glass jug. Mix well.
2 Fill 6 chilled cocktail glasses with crushed ice, pour the cocktail over the ice and serve at once.

Piña colada

MAKES 6 LONG DRINKS
700 ml/1¼ pints unsweetened pineapple juice
300 ml/½ pint canned coconut cream (see Buying guide)
350 ml/12 fl oz white or golden rum
plenty of crushed ice

1 Quarter fill a glass jug with ice, add one-third of the ingredients and mix briskly. Or blend for 2-4 seconds in a blender.
2 Pour into 2 chilled glasses and serve at once. Mix up 2 more batches with the remaining ingredients.

Planter's punch

MAKES 6 LONG DRINKS
350 ml/12 fl oz dark rum
175 ml/6 fl oz lemon juice
4 teaspoons grenadine
300 ml/½ pint orange juice
300 ml/½ pint pineapple juice
few dashes of Angostura bitters
plenty of crushed ice, to serve

TO GARNISH
6 orange slices
6 lemon slices
6 cocktail cherries

1 Put all the ingredients, except the ice, in a large glass jug and stir well.
2 Fill 6 large tumblers with crushed ice and pour the punch over the ice. Garnish each glass with an orange and lemon slice and a cherry.

Spicy coconut slices

MAKES ABOUT 25
1 small coconut
50 g/2 oz butter
large pinch of cayenne pepper
1 teaspoon salt

1 Make holes in 2-3 'eyes' of the coconut with a screwdriver, then drain off the 'milk'.
2 Give the coconut a sharp blow with a small hammer. Tap all the way round until the shell breaks. Break up the coconut into manageable pieces and dig out flesh with a knife. Cut flesh into neat slices.
3 Melt the butter in a large frying-pan, add the coconut and fry for 5 minutes until lightly coloured. Toss in the cayenne and salt to coat. Serve hot or cold.

Cook's Notes

Caribbean blues

TIME
5-10 minutes preparation in total.

COOK'S TIP
To make crushed ice: crush ice cubes in a strong blender or in a food processor. If you do not have either, place the ice in a strong polythene bag, squeeze out the air and tie. Wrap in a tea-towel and beat with a rolling pin.

● 160 calories/680 kj per glass

Piña colada

TIME
20 minutes preparation in total.

BUYING GUIDE
Canned coconut cream is available in some large supermarkets.

DID YOU KNOW
The name piña colada means soaked pineapple in Spanish.

● 365 calories/1530 kj per glass

Planter's punch

TIME
5 minutes preparation in total.

● 170 calories/720 kj per glass

Spicy coconut slices

TIME
The coconut takes about 15 minutes to prepare, then allow about 5 minutes for frying the slices and tossing in cayenne and salt.

● 20 calories/75 kj per slice

Sangria evening

Sangria, the refreshing Spanish wine cup, is just the thing for quenching thirsts in the heat of the summer. Full of fresh summer fruit and clinking with ice, this irresistible red wine cup will add a festive atmosphere to any informal gathering of friends.

Serve the drink accompanied by crunchy raw vegetables and a delicious cottage cheese and yoghurt dip, to help the evening go with a swing.

Sangria

SERVES 6

2 × 70 cl/1¼ pint bottles sweet red Spanish wine
5 fresh peaches, thinly sliced, or 400 g/14 oz can sliced peaches, drained
juice of 1 lemon
4 tablespoons brandy (optional)
1 eating apple
1 lemon
600 ml/1 pint soda water
ice cubes

1 Put the peaches in a large jug or glass bowl. Add the wine, lemon juice and brandy and allow to soak for about 2 hours.

2 Just before serving, slice the apple and lemon thinly and add to the jug with the soda water and ice cubes.

Cook's Notes

TIME
10 minutes to prepare, but allow 2 hours for the full flavour to develop.

●240 calories/1000 kj per portion

Crudités and dip

CRUDITÉS
SERVES 6
6 carrots
6 celery stalks
6 small or 3 large tomatoes
½ cucumber
8 radishes (optional)
1 small cauliflower

1 Top and tail, wash and scrape the carrots. Cut into thin sticks.
2 Wash celery and cut into sticks.
3 Cut large tomatoes into quarters, leave small ones whole.
4 Cut the tails off the cucumber and peel it if you prefer. Divide into 2 both lengthways and widthways. Cut each piece into 4 long strips.
5 Wash, top and tail the radishes.
6 Wash the cauliflower. Cut off the base then separate the head into florets. !
7 Arrange the crudités in groups around the edge of a tray, shallow basket or dish, leaving room for the dip in the centre.

COTTAGE CHEESE AND YOGHURT DIP

SERVES 6
225 g/8 oz cottage cheese
2 tablespoons natural yoghurt
2 spring onions or ½ onion
4 gherkins, finely chopped
salt and freshly ground black pepper
dash of Tabasco sauce (optional)

1 Sieve or blend the cottage cheese until smooth.
2 Add the yoghurt and mix well.
3 Wash and trim the spring onions. Chop finely and add to mixture.
4 Add finely chopped gherkins.
5 Season to taste and add Tabasco, if using.
6 Give a final mixing. Transfer to a serving bowl and place in centre of crudités.

Cook's Notes

 TIME
45 minutes to prepare the vegetables and make the dip.

 COOK'S TIP
Save time by preparing the dip in a blender. Blend all the ingredients except the onions and gherkins. Add these at the end and switch on for about 2 seconds so that they are only partially chopped into the dip.

 WATCHPOINT
If vegetables are prepared in advance store them in a plastic box or in the salad drawer of the refrigerator to avoid browning.

VARIATIONS
Use different varieties of vegetables such as red or green peppers, or raw button mushrooms.

● 45 calories/175 kj per portion

Cocktail party

Bring a touch of Hollywood to the long warm evenings of summer and invite your friends round to a genuine cocktail party. Choose one or two cocktails from the chart on page 116, offer them with our snacks, and your party is sure to be a wild success!

Mixing cocktails

The ingredients for cocktails are either stirred or shaken together. Traditionally, a cocktail shaker is used for shaking the ingredients, and many of these have built-in strainers, but rather than going to the expense of buying one specially for this occasion, you can easily improvise with a tight-lidded jar and a clean tea-strainer.

To shake a cocktail, put enough crushed ice into the shaker to cover the base to a depth of about 2.5 cm/1 inch. Then add the ingredients, shake and strain into the glass.

Crushed ice is often a vital ingredient of the drink — to prepare the ice, either crush ice cubes in a strong blender or food processor, or put ice in a strong polythene bag and crush with a wooden mallet or rolling pin.

A proper cocktail measure is very helpful, but a standard measuring jug and spoon can be used if ingredients are kept in the proportions given in the recipes. As a useful guide remember that 30 ml/ 1¼ fl oz equals 2 tablespoons.

The proportions given on page 116 are for one serving only.

Hot cheese and crab dip

SERVES 12

175 g/6 oz mature Cheddar cheese, grated
50 g/2 oz margarine or butter
50 g/2 oz plain flour
425 ml/¾ pint milk
1 tablespoon lemon juice
1 teaspoon Worcestershire sauce
1 teaspoon French mustard
salt and freshly ground white pepper
2-3 tablespoons finely chopped canned pimiento
2-3 tablespoons finely chopped green pepper
6 black olives, stoned and finely chopped
4 tablespoons dry white wine
175 g/6 oz canned crabmeat, drained and all cartilage removed

TO SERVE
small Melba toast squares
small cubes of French bread
small savoury biscuits

1 Melt the margarine in a saucepan, sprinkle in the flour and stir over low heat for 1-2 minutes until straw-coloured. Remove from the heat and gradually stir in the milk. Return to the heat and simmer, stirring, until thick and smooth.
2 Remove from the heat and stir in the cheese until melted and smooth. Add the lemon juice, Worcester-shire sauce, mustard and salt and pepper to taste and mix well.
3 Stir in the pimiento, green pepper, olives, wine and crabmeat, then heat through gently, stirring.
4 Pour into a warmed serving dish. Serve at once with small Melba toast squares, cubes of French bread and savoury biscuits (see Cook's tip).

Cook's Notes

TIME
10 minutes preparation; 10 minutes cooking.

COOK'S TIP
This dip is best if served piping hot. If possible, stand it on a warmed serving tray or hostess trolley.

● 160 calories/675 kj per portion

Chilli meat balls

MAKES 36-40

500 g/1 lb lean minced beef
2 tablespoons tomato ketchup
2 tablespoons mild chilli sauce
1 tablespoon Worcestershire sauce
25 g/1 oz cornflakes, finely crushed
125 ml/4 fl oz canned evaporated milk
salt and freshly ground black pepper
vegetable oil, for greasing

DIPPING SAUCE
5 tablespoons tomato ketchup
3 tablespoons mild chilli sauce
1 tablespoon lemon juice
¾ teaspoon creamed horseradish
¾ teaspoon Worcestershire sauce
few drops of Tabasco

1 Heat the oven to 200C/400F/Gas 6. Grease 2 baking trays with oil.
2 Place the beef in a large bowl together with the tomato ketchup, chilli sauce, Worcestershire sauce, cornflakes and evaporated milk. Season with salt and pepper to taste, then mix well together with your fingers.
3 Shape the beef mixture into about 40 bite-sized meat balls (see Cook's tip) and arrange on the greased baking trays. Cook in the oven for 15-20 minutes or until browned.
4 Meanwhile, make the sauce: put the tomato ketchup in a small serving bowl and stir in the rest of the sauce ingredients. Place the bowl of sauce in the centre of a large platter.
5 Serve the meat balls on a warmed serving dish accompanied by the dipping sauce (see Serving ideas).

COCKTAILS

COCKTAIL	INGREDIENTS	METHOD	TO SERVE
Gin-based:			
Boxcar	30 ml/1¼ fl oz gin 30 ml/1¼ fl oz Cointreau 1 teaspoon lime juice 1 egg white 1-2 dashes grenadine	Put all ingredients in shaker with crushed ice and shake well	First frost rim of champagne glass: dip glass into forked egg white and then caster sugar. Strain cocktail into glass
Gimlet	50 ml/2 fl oz gin 2 teaspoons lime juice cordial	Put ingredients in shaker with crushed ice and shake well	Strain into squat whisky glass and add ice cubes
Martini	50 ml/2 fl oz gin 1-2 teaspoons dry vermouth	Stir ingredients together	Serve in chilled cocktail glass garnished with an olive or twist of lemon rind
Bourbon or whisky-based:			
Horse's Neck	65 ml/2½ fl oz whisky few drops of lemon juice ginger ale	Stir whisky and lemon juice together, then add ice cubes and fill glass with ginger ale	Serve in tall glass garnished with a long spiral of lemon rind
Manhattan	65 ml/2½ fl oz whisky 25 ml/1 fl oz sweet vermouth	Stir ingredients together	Serve in cocktail glass garnished with maraschino cherry
Vodka-based:			
Black Russian	40 ml/1½ fl oz vodka 20 ml/¾ fl oz coffee liqueur	Put ingredients in shaker with crushed ice and shake well	Strain into squat whisky glass and add crushed ice
Bloody Mary	40 ml/1½ fl oz vodka 75 ml/3 fl oz tomato juice 1 tablespoon lemon juice dash of Worcestershire sauce few drops of Tabasco salt and black pepper	Put all ingredients in shaker with crushed ice and shake well. Strain and season to taste with salt and pepper	Serve in tall glass garnished with stick of cucumber and mint sprigs or lemon wedge
Harvey Wallbanger	25 ml/1 fl oz vodka orange juice 2 teaspoons galliano	Put vodka in glass, add ice cubes and fill with orange juice. Stir, then float galliano on top	Serve in tall glass
Rum-based:			
Between the sheets	25 ml/1 fl oz white rum 25 ml/1 fl oz brandy 25 ml/1 fl oz Cointreau 1 teaspoon lemon juice	Put all ingredients in shaker with crushed ice and shake well	Strain into squat whisky glass and add crushed ice
Daiquiri	50 ml/2 fl oz white rum 25 ml/1 fl oz lime juice 1 teaspoon sugar syrup	Put all ingredients in shaker with crushed ice and shake well	Strain into cocktail glass and add crushed ice
Tequila-based:			
Margarita	50 ml/2 fl oz tequila 2 teaspoons Cointreau 1 tablespoon lime juice	Place all ingredients in shaker with crushed ice and shake well	Frost rim of cocktail glass: dip glass into lime juice and then salt. Strain cocktail into glass
Tequila Sunrise	50 ml/2 fl oz tequila 125 ml/4 fl oz orange juice 2 teaspoons grenadine	Put tequila in glass, add ice cubes and fill glass with orange juice. Stir. Slowly pour in grenadine so it settles on bottom of glass	Serve in tall glass garnished with lemon slice. Stir cocktail before drinking

Sesame swizzles

MAKES 24-28
225 g/8 oz plain flour
salt and freshly ground black pepper
50 g/2 oz butter or margarine, diced
50 g/2 oz Gruyère cheese, finely
  grated
1 egg yolk
4 tablespoons water
75 g/3 oz sesame seeds
vegetable oil, for greasing

1 Sift the flour with a pinch of salt and pepper into a bowl. Rub in the butter, then stir in the cheese. Make a well in the centre.
2 Beat the egg yolk with water and pour into the well. Stir in with a fork, then gather the mixture together with your fingers, turn out on to a lightly floured surface and knead briefly to make a firm dough. Wrap in cling film and refrigerate for 10 minutes.
3 Heat the oven to 200C/400F/Gas 6. Lightly grease a large baking sheet.
4 Sprinkle half the sesame seeds on the work surface. Place the dough in the centre of the seeds and roll it out

to a rectangle measuring about 18 × 12.5 cm/7 × 5 inches.
5 Brush the surface very lightly with water, then sprinkle over the remaining sesame seeds. Roll the rolling pin over the dough to press the seeds in place.
6 Trim the edges with a sharp knife; cut lengthways into 12-14 strips.

Cut each strip across in half to make 24-28. Gently twist each strip into a swizzle shape (see Preparation).
7 Place the strips, slightly apart, on the prepared baking sheet. Bake in the oven for 15 minutes, until crisp and golden brown. Transfer to a wire rack and leave to cool completely (see Serving ideas).

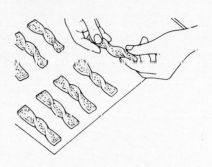

Champagne party

For a summertime celebration, splash out with an elegant Champagne party. Guests will be dazzled by the choice of heady Champagne cocktails, ranging from the classic brandy-flavoured cocktail, to the more full-bodied Black velvet, made with stout. Serve the cocktails with a tantalizing array of canapés to make a truly sophisticated affair.

Smoked salmon triangles

MAKES 40-48
5-6 large thin slices brown bread and butter, with crusts removed (see Preparation)

TOPPING
100 g/4 oz thinly sliced smoked salmon (see Cook's tip)
a little lemon juice
sweet paprika, to season
finely chopped fresh parsley, to garnish (optional)

1 Place the smoked salmon on top of the bread and butter so that it is completely covered.
2 Dip a stainless steel knife into lemon juice and spread lightly over each bread slice. Sprinkle evenly with a little paprika.
3 Using scissors, cut each slice of bread into 4 squares. Cut each square into 2 small triangles.
4 If garnishing the smoked salmon, dip the back of a stainless steel knife into lemon juice, then into the finely chopped parsley. Press down the centre of each of the smoked salmon triangles.

Cheesy pâté canapés

MAKES 36
4 slices pumpernickel (see Buying guide)
butter, for spreading

TOPPING
100 g/4 oz cream cheese
100 g/4 oz curd cheese
1 tablespoon soured cream
2 tablespoons snipped chives
salt and freshly ground black pepper

TO GARNISH
12 stuffed olives, sliced

1 Spread the pumpernickel with the butter to cover completely. ⚠ Cut each slice of pumpernickel into 9 squares to make 36 in all.
2 Beat the cheeses until smooth, then blend in enough soured cream to make a soft mixture suitable for piping. Add chives and season to taste with salt and pepper.
3 Spoon the pâté mixture into a piping bag fitted with a star nozzle and pipe a rosette on top of each square of pumpernickel.
4 Garnish with sliced olives.

Egg mayonnaise canapés

MAKES 36
4 large slices white bread, toasted and cooled
butter, for spreading

TOPPING
3 hard-boiled eggs
3-4 tablespoons thick bottled mayonnaise
salt and freshly ground black pepper

TO GARNISH
100 g/4 oz jar Danish lumpfish roe
sweet paprika

1 Trim the crusts off the cold toast, then spread with butter. Cut each slice into 3 each way, to make 9 small squares from each slice of bread – 36 squares altogether.
2 Chop the hard-boiled egg, then mix with the mayonnaise to bind. Season to taste with salt and freshly ground black pepper.
3 Pile small teaspoonfuls of the mixture on to the prepared toast squares and then garnish half with lumpfish roe and half with sweet paprika (see Cook's tip).

THE COCKTAILS
For a party lasting about 2 hours, allow 3-4 cocktails per person. One bottle of Champagne makes about 8 Champagne cocktails, so for a party of 25 people you will need 10-12 bottles of Champagne altogether.

To cut costs, use a good dry sparkling wine instead of Champagne. For best results, use a *méthode champenoise* sparkling wine, such as Saumur from France or Freixenet from Spain.

Champagne cocktail: place 1 lump of sugar in a saucer-shaped Champagne glass and sprinkle with 3-4 drops Angostura bitters. Leave for 1 hour until the sugar has dissolved, then add 1 tablespoon brandy and top up with chilled Champagne.
Buck's fizz: fill a tall Champagne glass (called a Champagne flute) one-third full with chilled freshly squeezed orange juice, then very carefully top up the glass with chilled Champagne.

Black Velvet: half-fill a 300 ml/½ pint lager or balloon glass with chilled Irish stout, then top up very carefully with chilled Champagne.
Champagne Framboise: pour 1 tablespoon Framboise (French raspberry-flavoured liqueur) into a tall Champagne glass. Top up very carefully with chilled Champagne.

Framboise gives a delicate pink colour and a mild, fruity taste; for a less expensive drink, use non-alcoholic raspberry syrup.

Cook's Notes

Smoked salmon triangles

TIME
About 20 minutes from start to finish.

COOK'S TIP
Make sure that the smoked salmon is very thinly cut or it will not cover sufficient slices. If it is a little thicker in parts press out lightly on greaseproof paper.

PREPARATION
To make thin slices of bread and butter, cut the crust off the end of an unsliced loaf, spread softened butter over the exposed bread surface, then cut off a thin slice. Repeat process to make 5-6 slices.

● 15 calories/75 kj per triangle

Cheesy pâté canapés

TIME
About 15 minutes to make and garnish.

WATCHPOINT
Butter pumpernickel well, to prevent the filling soaking into the bread.

VARIATION
Use mini-toasts as a base, and replace the cream and curd cheeses with 225 g/8 oz smooth liver pâté. Garnish with cocktail onions.

BUYING GUIDE
Pumpernickel is sold in packets and cartons in bread sections of supermarkets.

● 35 calories/150 kj per canapé

Egg mayonnaise canapés

TIME
10-15 minutes to prepare, plus extra time for the toast to cool.

DID YOU KNOW
Both red and black Danish lumpfish roe are available in jars from delicatessens. Lumpfish roe is often used as an inexpensive substitute for caviar, which it resembles. Use both colours for a stunning garnish.

COOK'S TIP
For best results, make the canapés less than 1 hour in advance or the toast will become rather tough.

● 40 calories/175 kj per canapé

INDEX